CHINA

By the staff of Editions Berlitz

How to use our guide

These 256 pages cover the main tourist destinations in China, arranged in alphabetical order for easy reference.

The **sights** to see are contained between pp. 53–199. Those most highly recommended are pinpointed by the Berlitz traveller symbol. The names of cities and top tourist attractions are printed in Chinese characters alongside the English equivalent—handy for trying to read signs or asking directions.

For **general background** see the sections The Land and the People p. 8, Facts and Figures p. 20, History p. 22 and The Arts p. 46.

Shopping, entertainment and **dining out** are described between pp. 200–215.

The **practical information,** hints and tips you will need before and during your trip begin on p. 216.

The **country map** at the beginning of the book (pp. 6–7) will give you an overall look at China, its provinces and main cities, while the **map section** at the back of the book (pp. 244–251) will help you find your way round and locate the principal sights.

Finally, if there is anything you cannot find, look in the complete **index** (pp. 252–256).

CONTENTS

CONTENTS

Acknowledgements

Text: Ken Bernstein

Layout: Doris Haldemann

Photos: Fernand Gigon pp. cover, 12, 23, 29, 40, 43, 46 (left), 51, 78, 83, 86, 103, 135, 139, 148, 152, 160, 166, 177, 201; Walter Imber pp. 10, 13, 16, 20, 29, 36, 38, 43, 46 (right), 47, 54, 60, 63, 68, 73, 79, 95, 97, 101, 106, 117, 122, 125, 130, 151, 155, 157, 164, 168, 172, 174, 182, 192, 193, 205, 206; Georg Stärk pp. 32, 52, 59, 70, 110, 149; Erwin Stegmann pp. 65, 127, 128, 143, 159, 167, 171, 203, 210, 214; Peter Jackson pp. 56, 71, 109, 179, 194, 213; Walter Vetsch pp. 58, 91, 132, 188; Ian Honeysett pp. 75, 90, 136, 199; China Travel & Tourism Press: pp. 84 Zhang Jiaqi, 113 Chen Shubo, 119, 145 Niu Songlin, 141 Xu Anning, 197 Liu Yingjie, 186.

We wish to express our thanks to the China Travel & Tourism Press, in particular Mr Lu Niangao, Deputy Director, and Mr Li Tiefei, Editor, for their invaluable help in the preparation of this guide. We are also grateful to the China International Travel Service (Luxingshe) for their cooperation.

Cartography: Falk-Verlag, Hamburg

S O V I E T
M O N G
Urumqi
Turpan
X I N J I A N G
Takli Makan Desert
Lop Nur
Dunhuang
G A N
Great Wall
Kunlun Mountains
Q I N G H A I
Indus
Himalayas
T I B E T (X I Z A N G)
Lhasa
Mount Everest 8848
N E P A L
BHUTAN
S I C
Jinsha R.
I N D I A
Ganges
INDIA
BANGLADESH
Kunming
YUNNAN
Salween
N
0 400 800 km
0 200 400 miles
Bay of Bengal
Irrawaddy
B U R M A
LAOS

U N I O N
O L I A
Gobi Desert
INNER MONGOLIA (NEI MONGOL)
HEILONGJIANG
Daqing
Harbin
Jilin
Changchun
JILIN
LIAONING
Shenyang
Anshan
DEM. PEOPLE'S REP. OF KOREA
SEA OF JAPAN
Chengde
Hohhot
Baotou
BEIJING
Shanhaiguan
Beidaihe
Dalian
Datong
HEBEI
Tianjin
Yantai
REP. OF KOREA
Great Wall
Taiyuan
Shijiazhuang
Hengshui
NINGXIA
SHANXI
Jinan
Qingdao
JAPAN
Yan'an
Yellow R.
Anyang
SHANDONG
Korea Strait
Lanzhou
Qufu
YELLOW SEA (HUANG HAI)
Kaifeng
Xi'an
Luoyang
Zhengzhou
JIANGSU
SHAANXI
HENAN
ANHUI
Yangzhou
Nanjing
Zhenjiang
Hefei
Wuxi
Yixing
Shanghai
HUBEI
Huang Shan
Suzhou
Chengdu
Yangtze (Chang Jiang)
Wuhan
1841
Hangzhou
Ningbo
EAST CHINA SEA (DONG HAI)
Leshan
ZHEJIANG
Chongqing
Jingdezhen
Yueyang
Nanchang
Okinawa
Changsha
JIANGXI
HUNAN
Fuzhou
Guiyang
FUJIAN
Taiwan Strait
GUIZHOU
Guilin
Xiamen
TAIWAN
Conghua Hot Springs
GUANGDONG
GUANGXI
Wuzhou
Guangzhou
Shenzhen
Foshan
Nanning
HONG KONG (under UK Admin.)
Taishan
Luzon Strait
VIETNAM
MACAO (under Port. Admin.)
SOUTH CHINA SEA (NAN HAI)
Gulf of Tongking
Hainan Island
PHILIPPINES
CHINA

THE LAND AND THE PEOPLE

Ancient, vast, evolving and exciting, China is the trip of a lifetime. The beauties, natural and man-made, vie for attention: mist-muffled hills silhouetted behind sampans on a winding river; proud pavilions of brilliant red and gold; the Great Wall undulating over ridges and mountains far into the distance; an elegant vase of eggshell-thin porcelain that has survived the centuries.

All the senses are engaged. Touch a two-thousand-year-old inscription in stone—or a bolt of newly woven silk. Taste the food of emperors. Listen to children singing. Smell the temple incense —or a fresh melon in the market-place.

Getting to China means crossing more than mere oceans and time zones. It's another world, culturally, linguistically and ideologically. Real disorientation sets in with a blur of tenses, present and past: ten minutes away from an ultra-modern hotel, water buffalo toil in the rice fields; to deliver half a ton of cabbage to market, a farmer and his son, harnessed, pull a primitive wagon; in a modern factory, artists copy thousand-year-old landscapes—for sale to tourists paying with credit cards.

The world's oldest living civilization can afford to be detached about time. It hasn't been very

Jutting limestone crags around Guilin create a dream landscape that is everyone's traditional image of China.

long, in the overall scheme of things, since the Chinese gave the world gunpowder and the compass, paper and printing, porcelain and silk. Putting history into perspective: the works of Confucius, the target of a book-burning binge in the 3rd century B.C., were again wildly controversial in the 1970s.

The most obvious source of dislocation for the newly arrived traveller is the language. More people can read Chinese than any other language on earth, but the visitor, bewildered by the elegant characters, finds this no consolation. And now they've gone and changed all the transcriptions, so Peking is Beijing and you can't remember whether you're going to Nanjing (formerly Nanking) or Nanning. And even if you make the supreme effort and try to speak, the tonal nuances usually foil the best will in the world.

Compounding the linguistic complications, the Chinese themselves speak a profusion of regional dialects; someone from the north can scarcely understand a word of Cantonese. To help everyone communicate, the government encourages the use of an official spoken language, *putonghua* (often known abroad as Mandarin), based on the Beijing dialect. Happily, no matter what dialect a Chinese uses in speech, the written language is universal. But then there are China's ethnic minorities, making up about 6 per cent of the population, who speak tongues as diverse as Mongolian and Miao, Thai and Tibetan. In parts of the sparsely settled western deserts and mountains, the minorities are the majority.

Language aside, the visitor's disorientation is further intensified by timeless "Chineseness" and the modern overlay of communism. Is the proliferation of polite but immovable bureaucrats a Marxist or a mandarin touch? Do families live three generations to an apartment because of tradition or the housing shortage? Why do Chinese infants almost never cry? Do they feel thoroughly loved or are they conditioned to be docile?

Every fourth child born into the world is Chinese. The well-known statistics come to life when you actually set foot in the most populous of all countries. At last report, China had 18 cities of more than one million inhabitants, and in any of them the bicycle rush hour is as hair-raising as a traffic jam in New York. In the most crowded province of all, Sichuan (Szechuan), you can journey for hours without ever

Sunshine or rain, it's all fun for these children of the Yi tribe, one of China's larger minority groups.

being out of sight of people or houses, even in the most remote rural areas.

As you travel the country by rail or air, you can't fail to be impressed by the intensive—human-intensive—agriculture. In the paddy fields you'll see hundreds of barefoot men and women collecting rice for processing in a single, hand-operated threshing machine. Everywhere, farmers work every inch of ground that isn't rock or sand or nearly vertical. When you subtract the mountains, deserts and other totally inhospitable terrain, only a small fraction—perhaps 15 per cent—of China's great land-mass is considered arable. Feeding everyone in China is a perennial preoccupation, a problem exacerbated by floods and drought.

The most mountainous part of the country is the western region, where highlands as forbidding as the Himalayas reach their apogee with Everest, on the China-Nepal border. (In the west, too, the desert descends to about 150 metres [500 feet] below sea level, so there's plenty of variety.) China's great rivers—the Yangtze, the Yellow and less legendary ones—rise in the west. Vast irri-

Tiles, blue as the sky, top the Temple of Heaven, where the emperor prayed for a good harvest.

13

gation projects have multiplied their effectiveness, and they produce hydro-electricity as a bonus. The rivers also electrify Chinese life with the periodic drama of their floods, some of which have figured among mankind's great disasters.

As you might expect of the world's third largest country (only the U.S.S.R. and Canada have greater areas), the weather blows hot and cold in China. It's about 5,800 kilometres (more than 3,000 miles) from northernmost China to the southern extremity, so while northerners are shovelling snow, southerners are sowing rice. Most of the rain falls in summer, and then mostly in southern and central China.

The bulk of China's 1,000-million-plus population lives in the east and south of the country, where a provincial town may have hundreds of thousands of inhabitants. Combining the world's most severe family-planning measures with restrictions on internal migration, the authorities have been trying to maintain the present level of urban versus rural population, by keeping the great majority down on the farm.

Nonetheless, the big cities are immense; Shanghai, with nearly 12 million citizens, may well be the world's biggest. Riding a bicycle to work across any of these cities can be a daily chore of one or two hours. And bikes are the mass transport of China. Private cars do not exist; taxis and official cars are few. This does not mean commuting is a fresh-air panacea. The bikes must share the roads with troops of heavy trucks and buses, noisy and chokingly smoky in the absence of exhaust controls.

The prospect of a long trek to the factory is only one of the possible disadvantages of big-city life. Housing is cramped and usually drab; shopping can be time-consuming and inconvenient. But life in town is much more comfortable, generally, than in the country; better facilities are available, from hospitals to schools. It's little wonder that many an ambitious villager dreams of the good life in urban society. But the government won't let him move to the city without a job.

The average wage is only about 60 yuan per month—what you might pay for an unexceptional dinner for four in a tourist hotel in Beijing. If the salary level seems disastrously inadequate, remember that the cost of living for

Inscrutable and intense, devotees of board games plot their moves.

15

Chinese is a small fraction of the Western equivalent. Rent may run a mere five yuan per month, and basic foods are cheap. In fact, some people have enough money left over to afford such local luxuries as wristwatches, tape recorders and television sets.

Wages fit into a scale system —usually eight grades. The "iron rice bowl" concept of assured income regardless of productivity has been much assailed in recent years, and discipline and incentives have now been added to spur hard work. (Though not at the expense of the daily siesta, which, as you might not have expected, is an established part of the Chinese work day.) Rewarding extra effort and good ideas with old-fashioned money is the sort of concept that ideologists battle over.

Incentives have also come to the rural scene, where the orthodox rigidity of centralized control has been relaxed. Peasant families are allowed to cultivate small private gardens and to raise their own pigs. By striving to better the output of the collective fields, they can now look forward to a share in the overall profits.

The production team (the bottom of the administrative pyramid) has been given more options and more possibilities of economic gain, including the chance to sell its handicrafts or surplus crops on the open market. The brigade, composed of up to several thousand people, handles such things as irrigation plans, setting up a light industry or a first-aid post. The top level of local control is a commune, which manages large-scale agricultural projects, negotiates production quotas with the government and runs schools and hospitals.

For the tourist, the utter strangeness of the organization of agriculture and industry adds much to the fascination of China. Responding to unending requests from visitors, tourism authorities routinely arrange excursions to factories and farms. There is no attempt to deny evident shortcomings. Nor do official guides disguise the fact that they are showing off model institutions of which the nation is proud, and not necessarily typical establishments. And if your tour group happens to be served a nine-course banquet at a collective farm's canteen, no one will try to convince you that this is the way ordinary farmers really live.

Such excursions are among the advantages of package tours to China. You may not know in advance—even one day in advance—what's on the agenda, but local tourism authorities try hard to organize varied and fulfilling programmes. Incidentally, there is no objection to foregoing any of these outings, but you should tell your guide in advance so everyone else doesn't lose time waiting for you.

Independent travel is a recent innovation in a country barely accustomed to the idea of group tourism; after all, tourists of any kind were almost unknown in China until the late 1970s. Facilities are still so limited that spur-of-the-moment travel is a chancy affair. But if you want to compose your own itinerary, and you don't mind losing time queueing up and trying to explain your problems at railway stations, airports and hotel reception desks, the adventure is appealing.

China's formal tourist attractions are so varied and so widely dispersed that a first trip can be little more than a preview. Even if time and money permit one of those grand tours of more than three weeks, you'll probably have to choose between a Yangtze River voyage and the Mogao Grottoes, or between the Stone Forest and the Silk Road.

Whatever your itinerary, you will experience the very diversity of China: in the morning, the sweeping roofs of a historic temple, in the afternoon a classic mountain panorama, and acrobatic performances or folk music in the evening. Somehow everyone manages to squeeze in three meals and some shopping, as well.

The food, most tourists agree, rates as an attraction in itself. Whether you're tucking into an official banquet or trying your luck at a neighbourhood noodle stall, there's really nothing like it anywhere else. Now is the time to sample all the classic recipes prepared with genuine ingredients in the time-honoured manner.

Souvenir shopping is a universal pastime, but the Chinese can hardly cope with the insatiable enthusiasm of so many foreign tourists; the authorities seem unable to open enough shops in enough tourist spots to satisfy the demand. Even so, you'll have abundant opportunities to look for antiques, ceramics, jade, rugs, silk and other potential bargains. Friendship Stores, run by the government, cater to foreigners and make shopping easy; polyglot personnel have the training and patience to meet any problem. But adventurous shoppers may just prefer neighbourhood department stores or outdoor markets where the local people sell handicrafts—even heirlooms.

After a long, hard day you may be tempted to opt out of the "nightlife" proposed on the timetable. All the same, summon up your strength and accept an invitation to the local cultural palace or theatre. This may be your only chance to see an authentic Peking Opera (or Cantonese Opera or Szechuan Opera—they are quite different), or acrobats daring the world from dizzying heights, or comics you laugh at without un-

T IS BETTER TO HAVE ONE CHILD ONLY

Putting policy into practice, China's 1,000 million limit births.

derstanding a word they say. Whatever the programme, it's bound to be full of insights into the latest cultural directives. The unadvertised stars of the show usually are the audience itself. They tend to be miserly with the applause, by the way, but don't let that inhibit you.

Even after you've seen all the historical, archaeological and artistic treasures, the cities and the breathtaking countryside, you can still find reasons to keep coming back to China. Some visitors do courses in acupuncture, for instance, or study Chinese martial arts, or Chinese Opera from the perspective of backstage. There are culinary package tours, as well; presumably the survivors

Babies, Ltd.

With their bright smiles and slit-bottomed trousers (for those little emergencies), Chinese toddlers are among the cutest in the world. But the stork brings only one to a family. And that's official.

Chinese parents with one child receive various benefits. If a second child is born, the privileges are revoked and social pressures are applied. The government begins assessing penalties if the number of children rises to three.

The restrictions—aimed at lowering China's alarming population growth rate—are particularly hard to enforce in the countryside, where farmers tend to look upon children as producers of wealth, and the more the better.

The government's "baby rationing" measures fly in the face of many Chinese traditions. The social and demographic repercussions—and infanticide is only one of them—are just beginning to be appreciated.

can rustle up Peking duck in their own kitchens.

The most unforgettable experience of China is being among the people. Just walk out of your hotel early in the morning and wade into the sea of China's 1,000 million people: there are waves of jingling bicycles, anxious throngs at bus stops, neighbours doing slow-motion callisthenics with pauses for gossip. Holding a bird-cage high, a pensioner takes his canary out for an airing. At a corner stall, Chinese snacks are prepared, sold and consumed.

How these people dress, work and relax never fails to fascinate the foreigner. Of course, the curiosity is more than reciprocated. You may sometimes feel uncomfortable, so avid is the attention you attract. But you couldn't want a friendlier welcome.

19

FACTS AND FIGURES

Geography: The area of China is nearly 9.6 million square kilometres (3.7 million square miles), slightly larger than the U.S.A. It is bordered (clockwise from the north) by the Mongolian People's Republic, the Soviet Union, North Korea, Vietnam, Laos, Burma, India, Bhutan, Nepal, India, Pakistan and Afghanistan. Sea frontiers: Bohai Gulf, Yellow Sea, East China Sea, South China Sea. About one-third of the country consists of mountains, reaching to the highest peak on earth — Mount Everest, at 8,848 metres (29,028 feet), known on the Chinese side of the Himalayas as Qomolangma. Of China's hundreds of rivers, the best known are the Yangtze and the Yellow.

Population: China's more than 1,000 million inhabitants make it the most populous country on earth. There are 56 nationalities, though the overwhelming majority of the people belong to the Han ethnic group.

Major cities: Shanghai, one of the world's largest cities, counts 11.9 million inhabitants. Beijing (Peking), the capital, has 9.2 million. Other cities among the world's biggest: Tianjin (Tientsin), Chongqing (Chungking) and Guangzhou (Canton).

Government: People's Republic led by the Chinese Communist Party and governed by the State Council, with legislation by the National People's Congress.

Economy: Centrally planned, socialist. Important natural resources: coal, iron, petroleum, copper. Major agricultural products: cotton, rice, wheat, soybeans. Principal exports: food products, textiles, minerals.

Religions: Traditionally, Buddhism, Daoism and Confucianism. Also Islam and (for a much smaller minority) Christianity.

Languages: More than 150 languages and dialects are spoken, but the official national language is the Mandarin form of Chinese. Though dialects vary considerably, the written language is universally understood.

THE IMPERIAL DYNASTIES

Xia (Hsia) Dynasty approx. 21st–16th centuries B.C.	First Chinese state evolves; silk produced; calendar devised.
Shang Dynasty 16th–11th centuries B.C.	Written language developed; bronze is cast.
Zhou (Chou) Dynasty 11th–5th centuries B.C.	Confucius and Lao-Tse; development of painting, poetry and mathematics.
Warring States 5th–3rd centuries B.C.	Navigational compass invented; iron tools in use.
Qin (Ch'in) Dynasty 221–206 B.C.	Great Wall built; weights and measures standardized.
Han Dynasty 206 B.C.–A.D. 220	Buddhism is introduced; paper invented; currency standardized.
Three Kingdoms A.D. 220–265	Tea-drinking is reported in Southern China.
Jin (Tsin) Dynasty A.D. 265–420	Luoyang's temples, palaces and library burned down by invaders.
Northern Dynasties A.D. 386–581	Construction of grottoes at Datong.
Southern Dynasties A.D. 420–589	China is invaded by Huns and Turks.
Sui Dynasty A.D. 581–618	Printing invented; Grand Canal construction project begins.
Tang (T'ang) Dynasty A.D. 618–907	Gunpowder invented; civil service examination resumed.
Five Dynasties and Ten Kingdoms A.D. 907–960	Money economy encourages expansion of trade in China.
Song (Sung) Dynasty A.D. 960–1280	Movable-type printing; paper currency in circulation.
Yuan Dynasty A.D. 1279–1368	Marco Polo in China in service of Kublai Khan; first world atlas.
Ming Dynasty A.D. 1368–1644	Beijing's Imperial Palace built; Great Wall restored.
Qing (Ch'ing or Manchu) Dynasty A.D. 1644–1911	Rebellions, Opium Wars, decline of the monarchy.

HISTORY

Hundreds of thousands of years before China was to become the world's longest-running civilization, the prologue was enacted in the flicker of a carefully tended fire: Peking Man, a forbear of Homo Sapiens, achieved a mastery of fire—we could call it the first Chinese invention. Not that he devised flint and steel or matches or any other way of *creating* fire. Peking Man simply learned how to capture flame, perhaps from a forest fire, and keep it alight. He thus enjoyed two revolutionary luxuries: light and heat.

Technologically and sociologically it was a phenomenal breakthrough, meaning that communities could live year-round in one cave, where cooking, even smelting could be pursued. And so, by 400,000 B.C., about 50 kilometres south-west of present-day Beijing, the ancestors of mankind were ready to settle down. (Several hundred thousand years later, when Marco Polo reached the capital of China, he was astonished by a further sophistication of fire. The Chinese, he announced, used "black stones", dug out of mountains, as fuel—Europeans had not yet invented the word "coal", nor discovered a use for it.)

The confluence of mythology and history in China occured around 4,000 years ago in what is referred to as the Xia (Hsia) Dynasty. This was still the Stone Age, but the people are even thought to have made silk from thread produced by the worms they cultivated on the leaves of their mulberry trees.

During the second of the quasi-legendary dynasties, the Shang (about the 16th to 11th centuries B.C.), the Chinese developed an interest in art. Careful geometric designs, as well as dragon and bird motifs, adorned bowls and implements. And with the arrival of the Bronze Age, the Chinese created bronze vessels of such beauty and originality that, until modern times, archaeologists refused to believe they were cast 3,000 years ago.

The Shang Dynasty gave rise to the concept of one Chinese nation under one government. Another Shang innovation was a written language, originally used by oracles and then official scribes—China's first scholars. Among advances of the era were the introduction of astronomical calculations, chariots, cowrie shells as a unit of exchange, the construc-

Courting luck: arms outstretched, eyes closed, a woman reaches to touch an ancient ideogram.

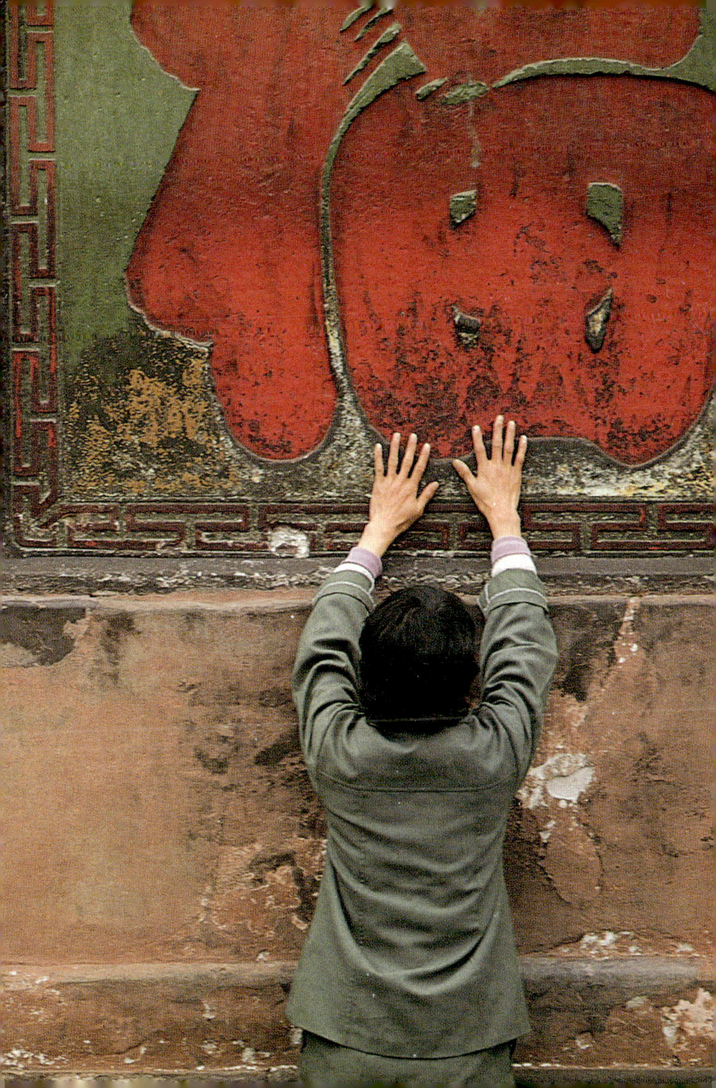

tion of palaces and temples, and the refinement of table manners through the use of chopsticks.

The most durable dynasty in Chinese history followed the Shang: the Zhou (Chou), which kept power from around the 11th to 5th centuries B.C. Chinese boundaries were expanded, land reform was instituted, and towns were built. But perhaps more significantly, the declining years of the Zhou era produced two of China's most influential thinkers.

In the rest of the world, China's supreme sage, Kong Fuzi (K'ung Fu-tzu), is known by the Latinized name of Confucius. He was born in 551 B.C. in what is now Shandong Province in eastern China. So profound was his influence that eleven Chinese emperors made pilgrimages to the birthplace of the Great Teacher. You, too, can pay your respects at the vast temple raised on the site of his home in the small town of Qufu (Chufu), and at his tomb in the woods just to the north.

The classics of Confucius set ideals for human and political relations, establishing precepts for succeeding generations of Chinese intellectuals. Like biblical scholars, they perused his every word for every nuance, an exercise that profoundly affected centuries of Chinese rulers and civil servants. Curiously, in spite of the subtleties he propounded, Confucius virtually never delved into the supernatural or explored the mystical and spiritual thoughts that occupied the renowned thinkers of the major religions.

Over the centuries Confucius has suffered more changes of fortune than probably any other philosopher. Honoured soon after his death as the greatest of scholars, he was later revered as semi-divine, then reduced to the status of most highly respected of all thinkers. During the Cultural Revolution in the 1970s, Confucius was reviled as a counter-revolutionary force, but he has since been rehabilitated as the humanist whose ideas influenced the cultures of China, Japan, Korea and Vietnam.

Unlike Confucius, about whose life many specific and even colourful details are known, the philosopher Laozi (Lao Tse or Lao-Tzu) is something of an unknown quantity in personal terms. Estimates of his date of birth vary by well over a century. One legend says he taught the young Confucius. Laozi is immortalized by a book of thoughts on man, nature and the universe which inspired the creed later named Daoism (Taoism). With its emphasis on spirit worship, passivity in the face of cosmic forces, and "knowledge which is not knowledge", Daoism became the most authentically Chinese religion.

A Galaxy of "Firsts"

Few people realize just how many inventions first saw the light in China, often centuries before they reached the West. Here are just a few:

The Chinese began making **paper** in the 1st century A.D., by pulping rags and wood fibre; it took a thousand years for the technique to reach Europe.

Block **printing** was known in China in the 9th century and movable type came in to use a couple of hundred years later; printing was not invented in Europe until 1440.

Excavations show that the Chinese were producing **cast iron** in the 4th century B.C.—some 18 centuries before Europe discovered the art.

The Chinese were the first to build **suspension bridges,** combining bamboo and wrought-iron chains.

Indians thought up the toe-stirrup (suitable for bare feet), but the Chinese invented the **foot-stirrup,** which revolutionized warfare by enabling horsemen to control their mounts while using both hands to fire a cross-bow.

Paddle-boats, operated by a treadmill, plied Chinese waterways 1,300 years ago.

The simple device of the wheelbarrow, ideal for narrow paths through fields and alongside canals, first appeared in China in the 3rd century; it took a thousand years to reach Europe.

Mechanical clocks, powered by a water-wheel, were in use in China from A.D. 700 onwards. Water was also used in association with **driving-belts, chain-drives** and **cranks,** all Chinese inventions, in early textile and winnowing machinery.

The **magnetic compass** was another first—though the West later made greater use of it to circumnavigate the world.

The Chinese discovered **gunpowder** and used it to propel arrows from bamboo tubes to produce the first **rockets**—an invention that ultimately led man to the moon.

A more soothing discovery was **tea,** and the Chinese soon raised its cultivation, processing and infusion to a fine art. As early as the 8th century a Chinese connoisseur wrote: "The best quality leaves must have creases like the leathern boot of a Tatar horseman, curl like the dewlap of a mighty bullock, unfold like a mist rising out of a ravine, gleam like a lake touched by a zephyr, and be wet and soft like fine earth newly swept by rain".

And at least 200 years before vaccination was developed in Europe, Chinese physicians were practising **immunization** by placing material from a smallpox pustule in a patient's nostril.

While China's intellectual vanguard was marching inexorably forward under the banners of order and harmony, the nation's political life staggered and stumbled towards chaos. The disintegration of the Zhou Dynasty led to the 250-year period known as the age of the Warring States. Orthodox Communist histories make the advent of this era the dividing line between a "slave society" and a "feudal society". For a convenient date, they use the year 475 B.C.

The Chinese Empire

The term "China" is a relatively recent innovation, believed to be derived from the designation of the first dynasty after the Warring States, the Qin (Ch'in). The name China was probably coined by foreigners, for the Chinese themselves had no need for any other label than the obvious, ethnocentric description of their country: the Middle Kingdom.

Under Qin rule (221–206 B.C.) the empire was organized along strict and altogether efficient lines. Land was divided into provinces and prefectures, with power devolving on a central government staffed by highly educated bureaucrats. Disapproved books were burned and dissidents executed or exiled. Canals, roads and the Great Wall were built under the auspices of an extensive public works programme, staffed mostly by conscripts. Official decrees standardized weights and measures and even the axle dimensions of all wagons (the latter edict kept transport in the same ruts for countless years).

Nowadays trucks, instead of camels, travel the Silk Road, the fabled trade route across Central Asia.

The great Han Dynasty (206 B.C.–A.D. 220), which followed the Qin, carried progress one step further. Civil servants were selected by competitive exams, the government issued all coinage and standardized currency, the "Silk Road" across central Asia opened up trade with the rest of the world.

On the military front, the Han triumphed over marauding Huns and Central Asian nomads, and Chinese sovereignty was extended almost to today's frontiers. The development of a new crossbow—a longer-range, more accurate weapon than China's foes could deploy—ensured Han supremacy.

A golden age ensued. A university was established in the capital city, Chang'an (now Xi'an). Intellectuals, who had been harried by the Qin, were encouraged to create; with the invention of paper, the influence of their writings spread. Sculpture, ceramics and silk manufacture flourished. And a new religion came to China from India via Tibet — Buddhism. It was to have an enduring effect on Chinese life and art.

Like dynasties before and after, the Han succession ended in a rattle of battle, in demoralization, mutiny, power struggle and anarchy. The nation was split into three kingdoms, which fought among themselves.

The era of the Three Kingdoms lasted only about half a century. The period has as a legacy some thrilling tales of derring-do that later inspired various plays and a classic Ming-Dynasty novel. And the first mention of tea drinking in China occurs in the 3rd century, a footnote of fascination for social historians.

Over the next several hundred years a series of dynasties, some headed by foreign rulers, held power under almost constant threat from usurpers at home and abroad. During this unsettled period many people moved to the south; the Yangtze valley developed into the leading centre of Chinese culture. As for foreign invaders, they brought new ideas. But, as often happened in Chinese history, they were assimilated into the more advanced society of the Middle Kingdom.

National unity and strength were renewed under the Sui Dynasty (A.D. 581–618), a brief prelude to the highest achievements of Chinese art. The Sui built a stately new metropolis at Chang'an, near the site of the old Han capital. They also began work on the Grand Canal, which was to link the rice-bowl of the Yangtze valley with Beijing, an engineering achievement comparable to the construction of the Great Wall.

The Glory of the Tang

In the realm of culture, no era of Chinese history has surpassed the Tang (T'ang) Dynasty (618–907). Poetry and art reached a brilliant apex. China's Imperial Academy of Letters was founded — about 900 years before any such institution was established in Europe. The first known printed book, a Buddhist scripture, was published in China in A.D. 868.

The capital city, Chang'an, had a population of more than a million — far bigger than any European city of the age. Extravagant palaces and temples alternated with markets stocked with exotica from as far away as Byzantium.

For 2,000 years the Great Wall guarded China's northern frontier against marauders. Today it's a top tourist attraction.

28

A statue in Hangzhou's Yue Fei Temple commemorates the popular 12th-century general who was betrayed and murdered in prison.

Foreign traders journeyed here to purchase silk, porcelain and spices—incidentally introducing the Chinese to foreign concepts.

Scholars, poets and artists achieved prominence. Encyclopedias were compiled. Poetry evolved a tonal pattern and lines that rhymed. As Buddhism gained strength and took on a Chinese character, it inspired the construction of great temples adorned with frescoes and statues. Artists also painted sensitive landscapes and perfected the subtle brushwork of calligraphy. Sculptors outdid themselves in portraying lifelike humans and animals and religious figures.

Yet by the beginning of the 10th

century, the Tang rulers had lost their grip on the country. Tax collections dwindled, ambitious palace eunuchs plotted, reform schemes failed, rebellious forces threatened. The emperors distributed their largesse to too many warlords, hoping to pacify them. By 907 the people could see, through all the turmoil and confusion, that the dynasty had lost the Mandate of Heaven, and so it was that the last of the Tang monarchs abdicated.

Chinese historians designate the next 50 years as the era of "The Five Dynasties and the Ten Kingdoms". This transitional period was marred by political and military infighting, by rivalry, intrigue and cruelty.

However, when Europe was still in the Dark Ages, an able general, Zhao Kuang-yin (Chao K'uang-yin) came onto the scene and founded the Song (Sung) Dynasty (960–1280), which ensured Chinese cultural supremacy for the next three centuries.

The number of cities in China increased dramatically under the Song, mostly in the Yangtze valley and in the south-east. And where there were cities, there were scholars, artists and artisans. Movable type revolutionized printing, books became more common and literacy increased. Chinese scientists published works on botany, astronomy, mathematics and geography. The emperors appointed official court painters. Glazed porcelain was received abroad with admiration and awe.

But while art and scholarship continued to thrive, the political and military situation deteriorated under the Song. Foreign invaders chipped away at the fringes of the empire. Taxpayers groaned under the burden of the army and the tribute paid to foreign rivals and complained at having to support the luxuries of palace life.

Disaster was inevitable: invaders from Manchuria forced the Song to retreat to the south. And the terrible Mongol hordes, led by the redoubtable Genghis Khan, swept across China, bringing the whole country under foreign rule for the first time.

Under Mongol Rule (1279–1368) A poignant drama signalled the Mongol conquest of China. After 20 years of resistance, the Song armies were finally ready to capitulate. The boy emperor was hidden aboard a ship. But when it was surrounded by enemy craft, the last of the loyal commanders seized the eight-year-old monarch in his arms and leaped with him to death in the sea.

The new era, known as the Yuan Dynasty, lasted less than a century. Creativity declined, but the new ruler of China, Kublai Khan (the grandson of the great

31

Genghis Khan), had an open mind and a generally humane attitude towards his new subjects. He appointed Chinese bureaucrats and scholars to help rule the country. Foreign historians generally conclude that Kublai Khan became an almost authentic Chinese emperor, that the conquerors changed more profoundly than the conquered.

The capital of the new Mongol/Chinese Empire was built on the site of present-day Beijing and called Cambaluc—or Kanbalu, as it was spelled by that most renowned of medieval travellers, Marco Polo. His account of the vast, new capital throbs with admiration for the palaces, the bazaars and the profusion of shade trees. He regards with wonder the Great Khan's religious tolerance, all-encompassing generosity—as well as his admirable taste in wives. He discovers all manner of innovations, not least the invention of paper money. (Counterfeiting, he reports, was treated as a capital offence.)

Marco Polo's account of life in legendary Cathay was received with incredulity in Europe, where it was suggested that his imagination had run wild. What else were the citizens of Venice to make of his report that the "noble and magnificent city of Kin-sai" (now Hangzhou) had 12,000 bridges, many so high that sailing ships could pass under them. In England, schoolboys came to call a whopping exaggeration a "Marco Polo".

With the death of Kublai Khan (in 1294 at age 80), the Mongols started to lose their grip on China. The great emperor's successors lacked his vision and vigour. Insurrection was in the air, met by oppression, resulting in ever more sustained resistance. Finally, a full-scale uprising led by a peasant general, Zhu Yuanzhang (Chu Yüan-chang), routed the Yuan rulers. In 1368 Zhu Yuanzhang assumed the throne of the Middle Kingdom, founding yet another dynasty of brilliant promise—the Ming.

The Elegance of Ming (1368–1644) In Chinese, the word "Ming" is written as a composite of the characters for "sun" and "moon", combined to mean "brilliant" or "glorious". In actual fact the dynasty didn't quite live up to its name.

Beauty was achieved in architecture, sculpture and the decorative arts. But literature, now serving an ever-wider audience, produced few master works. Philosophy saw no new developments. Science, which had been far more advanced than in Europe, was so gravely neglected that China became a technological backwater.

Perhaps to compensate for the Mongol interlude, the Ming emperors opted for traditional Chinese values. The keeper of the Mandate of Heaven played his role to the autocratic hilt, while bureaucrats kept their jobs—and heads—by paying him lip service.

Conservatism and hostility to foreign ideas couldn't be absolute, however. During the Ming era China managed to import tobacco, pineapples, peanuts and syphilis. Thanks to the emancipated Confucian tradition, Christian missionaries were generally welcomed, though they hardly achieved mass conversions. From the Jesuits the Chinese learned mathematics, astronomy, and how to adapt the skill of bronze-casting to the production of heavy cannon.

At first the Ming headquarters was moved south to the Yangtze River port of Nanjing ("Southern Capital"), but at the beginning of the 15th century the capital returned to what was now renamed Beijing ("Northern Capital"). Here Ming architects and artisans produced some of China's most elegant palaces, temples and parks.

The move northward made easier the supervision of defence efforts on the ever sensitive borders of the empire. This proved ironic in the 17th century. After repeated forays, infiltrations and invasions, forces from Manchuria capitalized on domestic upheavals in China to take power in Beijing, almost by default. Consolidating control over the rest of the country, though, was a long, brutal business. The Manchu invaders called their new dynasty the Qing (Ch'ing). Fated to be the last of all the Chinese dynasties, it held power until modern times (1644–1911).

Pigtails and Prosperity

The invading "barbarians", the Manchu, adopted all the refinements of Chinese civilization, installing a regime so conservative that it began to hold back progress. But for all their Confucian outlook and traditionalism, the Manchu imposed one singular feature of their own culture—the wearing of pigtails. Ironically, this was one peculiarity the rest of the world came to consider typically Chinese.

One of the most dynamic emperors was Kang Xi (K'ang-hsi), whose reign roughly coincided with that of Louis XIV of France. He presided over a period of prosperity and positive achievement, rebuilding Beijing, encouraging scholarship, expanding the empire to its greatest area. By the standards of his predecessors, Kang Xi lived modestly enough; his concubines numbered no more than 300.

Under Kang Xi's grandson, the Emperor Qian Long (Ch'ien Lung), conflict arose between Europe's empires and the Middle

Kingdom. England's King George III sent an emissary to negotiate conventional diplomatic and trade relations. The emperor flatly turned him down but thanked him for showing such "submissive loyalty in sending this tribute mission". No insult appears to have been intended, even though the message referred to England as "the lonely remoteness of your island, cut off from the world by intervening wastes of sea".

China sincerely believed that it was the centre of the world, that it had nothing to learn or gain from so-called foreign devils. But such sublime self-assurance was to be short-lived.

The soaring demand in Europe for Chinese tea, silk and porcelain brought increasing pressure for freer trade. But the Chinese were adamant. Needing no commodities, they would accept only silver bullion in exchange, undermining Britain's balance of payments. Then, around the turn of the 19th century, wily traders thought of an alternative medium of payment—opium.

In 1839 the Chinese government finally cracked down on this drain on the treasury, which was also causing mass addiction. Some 20,000 chests of opium were confiscated from British merchants in Guangzhou (Canton). Retaliation came a year later, in the first of the Opium Wars, which culminated in a series of

Soaring against a backdrop of modern apartment and office blocks, the Temple of Heaven dominates the Beijing skyline.

"unequal treaties" forced on an ever-weaker Manchu regime. China was obliged to open major ports to foreign political and economic penetration; Hong Kong was ceded to Britain.

Infinitely more costly in human terms was the Taiping Rebellion, which began in 1850 as a peasant revolt. The struggle between the Qing Dynasty and rebels determined to overthrow traditional values—a respect for religion, private property and male supremacy—lasted 14 years and cost more lives than World War I. The Beijing government finally won, but the regime and the nation would never be the same.

This became patently clear during the Sino-Japanese War of 1894-95, in which the inadequacy of the Chinese army was starkly displayed. Japan and Western

powers were dismantling the Chinese Empire. Demands for reform won the support of the emperor, but his notoriously scheming aunt, the Empress Dowager Ci Xi (Tz'u Hsi), edged him off the throne.

Soon afterwards, Ci Xi had the chance to exploit the Boxer Rebellion (1900), a revolt against foreign influence. It was finally put down by the intervention of all the great powers, which joined together in an unprecedented alliance. China was saddled with payment of a humiliating indemnity; the Mandate of Heaven was tottering.

The elderly empress died in 1908, one day after the mysterious death of her nephew, the unseated emperor. The heir apparent was a two-year-old prince — hardly the leader the dynasty and the nation needed in the face of civil disorder and foreign threats. Less than three years later, an army uprising in Wuhan, the capital of Hubei Province, quickly won widespread support. The success of the revolution surprised many observers. Even Dr. Sun Yat-sen, the inveterate revolutionary who had led several earlier insurrections, was abroad at the time. He returned in triumph to accept the presidency of the Chinese Republic. With a stroke of the brush, the Manchu Dynasty and its child-emperor surrendered. Imperial tradition going back thousands of years was snapped like a twig.

Buddhism flourished for centuries in China, leaving its impact on literature and art. The religion lives on today in the great temples and sculptures and in the handful of monks that maintain them.

Unity Eludes the Chinese

But the path of the new republic was strewn with dangers. A warlord seized power in Beijing, hoping to restore the monarchy. A harried Sun Yat-sen moved his new Kuomintang party south to Guangzhou.

Towards the end of hostilities, China entered World War I on the side of the Allies. But the Versailles Peace conference proved a bitter disappointment when Japan, not China, won control over Germany's former holdings in Shandong Province. Frustration inspired protest demonstrations. The targets of increasing bitterness were the foreign powers and the regime in Beijing. Agitation for drastic social reforms caught the imagination of students and factory workers.

In 1921, the Communist Party of China (with a total membership of 53) held its first national congress, in secret, in Shanghai. A cautious Communist alliance with the Nationalist Party (Kuomintang or KMT) was agreed on in 1924. Disappointed with the Western powers, Dr. Sun Yat-sen turned for support to the leaders of the young Soviet regime. The Kremlin obliged, sending political and military advisors to the Nationalists. In turn, Dr. Sun dispatched his 37-year-old follower, Chiang Kai-shek, as head of a mission to Moscow. Dr. Sun, who rallied the Chinese behind his Three Principles—Nationalism, Democracy and the People's Livelihood—died in 1925. His successor, Chiang Kai-shek, took over the campaign, moving the capital to Nanjing.

In 1927 Chiang turned on the Communists as well as left wingers within his own KMT, unleashing a vehement bloody purge. The Communists, who had already organized millions of peasants, gathered strength in the south. But under increasing military pressure, they set forth on the epic Long March to north-west China—10,000 perilous kilometres (more than 6,000 miles) in one of history's great strategic retreats. Along the way, one of the founders of the Chinese Communist Party, Mao Zedong (Mao Tse-tung), was chosen as party leader—a mandate he retained for the rest of his life.

The Bitter Years of War

In 1931 Japan seized Manchuria, proclaiming it the "independent" state of Manchukuo—a fatal prologue to World War II. Over the next few years Japanese troops advanced into several other areas of northern China. The government of Chiang Kai-shek was so busy tracking down the Communists that the Japanese foe merited only casual attention. At one point Chiang himself was kidnapped by some of his own officers—a sensational interlude known as the Sian (Xi'an) Incident—to convince him to form a united front with the Communists.

But by the time concerted action could be planned, the invaders had moved onto a broad offensive. The Japanese juggernaut crushed all the resistance in the big coastal cities, as well as Beijing and Nanjing. The KMT retreat ended in 1938 with the Nationalist government dug in behind the gorges of the Yangtze River, in the last-ditch capital of Chongqing.

Even before entering World War II, the United States supported the armies of Chiang Kai-shek with food, fuel and transport. However, Americans in the field soon became disheartened with the confusion, corruption and stalling. Chiang, they believed, was hoarding everything from rice to airplanes for the struggle against the Chinese Communists, and letting the Allies worry about the Japanese.

When Japan surrendered in 1945, Chiang Kai-shek could share the victory toasts as one of the Allies. But he was already losing the battle of his lifetime—for China.

By V-J Day, when Japan was defeated, the Chinese Communists controlled an area inhabited by nearly one-quarter of the nation's population. At first the Americans tried to mediate between the Communists and the KMT regime, even while continuing to supply the Nationalists. But chances for post-war cooperation between right and left were wrecked in a matter of months: China was sinking into the tragedy of civil war.

Despite some early setbacks, the Communist armies became an overwhelming force, once they had regrouped. They were greeted as liberators by the peasants and met only desultory resistance in most cities. The Nationalists, in despair, fell back. Finally, the key figures of the KMT regime, as well as a multitude of political refugees, fled the country. They moved the Nationalist government and countless national treasures to the island of Taiwan, pledging to fight their way back one day.

In Beijing's Tian An Men Square on October 1, 1949, the Party Chairman Mao Zedong proclaimed the People's Republic of China. After thousands of years of empire and a few decades of violent transition, the most populous country in the world was committed to communism.

Imposing the New Order

Before any grandiose plans could be implemented, China's new rulers had to rebuild society and a crippled economy. Agrarian reform was the first revolutionary innovation, followed by the orga-

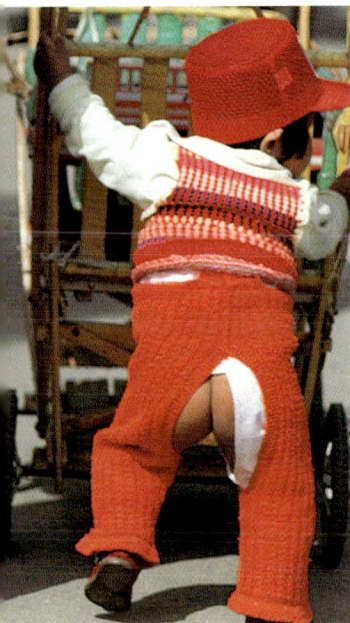

nization of the cities under Party control.

Hardly had the groundwork been laid when China entered the Korean War, sending "volunteers" to fight against American-led United Nations forces. U.S.-China relations scarcely surmounted this tense nadir for some 20 years. Beijing's ties with Moscow, however, prospered in comradely harmony. The world's first communist state, the U.S.S.R. shipped technical advisors and roubles to China, which patterned many new institutions on Soviet models. As in Russia, farms were collectivized and heavy industry took economic precedence. But in the late 1950s the Chinese rejected the Stalinist model and began the search for new prototypes.

Mao Zedong's "Great Leap Forward", designed to mobilize the masses in a crash programme of economic growth, kept the country in turmoil and brought unconvincing results, at best. About the time the Leap was suddenly reversed, relations between China and the Soviet Union plunged from polite to frosty to hostile. Meanwhile, China had tested its own nuclear bomb.

From 1966 to 1976, China was convulsed by the Great Proletarian Cultural Revolution. Millions of young Red Guards went on the rampage, and the whole country set about memorizing the maxims of Mao. Thousands perished and much of China's artistic heritage was destroyed as a vestige of feudalism.

Not an inch of land goes to waste: apartment-dwellers tend urban allotments.

Changes came in quick succession in the 1970s. Defence Minister Lin Biao died in 1971 — ostensibly in a plane crash — as he fled from a foiled attempt to seize power. U.S. President Richard Nixon visited China, normalizing relations between the two countries. The widely admired prime minister, Zhou Enlai, died. Eight months later, in September 1976, death came to Chairman Mao himself.

Mao's widow, the one-time film actress Jiang Qing, and her close associates (the so-called Gang of Four) were arrested, tried and imprisoned for stirring up the excesses of the Cultural Revolution. Thousands who had suffered during the fervid 1960s and '70s — including the forceful pragmatist Deng Xiaoping — were rehabilitated. As Mao Zedong's portraits and slogans were removed from signboards and

---

The New Vernacular
Foreigners are often baffled by the terminology used by their local guides. It's English, but what does it mean? A few typical expressions:

Barefoot doctor. *Peasant trained as a paramedic.*
Cadre *(pronounced KAH-derr). A Communist Party activist or a civil servant.*
Eight Imperialist Powers. *Austria, Britain, France, Germany, Italy, Japan, Russia, U.S.A. — whose armies intervened in China in 1900.*
Hegemonism. *One country's effort to dominate another, sometimes describing Soviet policies.*
Hundred Flowers. *Phase in 1957 when government invited criticism; critics were later punished as dissenters.*
Liberation. *Establishment of Chinese People's Republic (1949).*
Modernization. *General policy of strengthening economy with pragmatic methods.*
Overseas Chinese. *Anyone of Chinese descent who lives abroad, regardless of birthplace or citizenship.*
Pinyin. *Official system of reproducing Chinese language in Roman letters.*
P.L.A. *People's Liberation Army (Chinese army).*
Politburo. *Ruling council of Communist Party.*
Re-education. *Euphemism for treatment of dissidents.*
Unequal Treaties. *19th-century concessions forced on weak Manchu government by foreign powers.*

schoolrooms, a new flexibility came to the fore. At the expense of the hard-line dogmatists, top priority was assigned to the modernization of China's admittedly underdeveloped economy—by any effective means. This opened the way for major scientific and commercial exchanges with the West.

And foreign tourists soon began flooding in to see the splendours which had been inaccessible for so long. In one important respect, nothing had changed—not, for that matter, since the time of Marco Polo. China was still one and only, a country like no other.

China looks to the future as bikes keep the wheels of industry turning.

The People's Commune

China's farmers have a fraction of the world's farmland to work—and more than 20 per cent of the planet's people to feed. The soil is often unproductive, the climate capricious and the population forever growing. A drought or typhoon can still upset the balance between the supply of food and the demand, however modest each individual's requirements. Every square inch of usable land, including plots that seem impossibly arid or inaccessible, has to be exploited to the very limit—regardless of the scarcity of tractors and trucks, pumps and pipes. The problem is certainly not new—but the solutions adopted are.

When the Communists came to power in 1949, 10 per cent of the population owned 70 per cent of the land. High costs, low yields and mismanagement had made farming uneconomic. Realizing that the people and the land were the country's most vital assets, the new regime set out to reorganize agriculture along more profitable lines. While allowing peasant smallholders to retain their property, the authorities redistributed the bulk of the land, confiscated from wealthy landlords, among the previously landless masses. Slowly, over a period of years, a new agricultural order evolved.

To begin with, mutual aid teams were formed in which labour, draught-animals and implements were pooled. The next step was the development of cooperatives. Land, animals and tools were held in common and income was shared. Sometimes as many as 200 families from one or more villages would join forces. Revenue would be collectively owned and invested for the welfare of all. Finally, cooperatives were merged into an even larger unit, the commune, a group of villages and outlying hamlets responsible for local agricultural and industrial enterprises, commerce, education and home defence. By the end of 1958, virtually every peasant family was part of a people's commune.

Today there are over 90,000 such communes, with an average of 9,000 members. Within the commune there is a clearly defined hierarchy. The production brigade, manned by representatives of various villages, oversees operations, while the central economic unit, the production team (fifteen to thirty families) takes charge of a crop and owns most of the land on which it is grown. The family provides the foundation for the entire system. Families live in their own homes and are allowed to cultivate small private plots and rear pigs and chickens for their personal profit.

After the commune has met its responsibilities to the state and expenses are deducted, earnings and revenue are divided up among members according to the work-point system, in which each task is allotted a specific number of points by the team as a whole.

If you have the chance to visit a people's commune, don't miss it. After all, it is the way of life of 80 per cent of China's population. You may have imagined a commune as some sort of barracks compound where the members dine in a mess hall. Instead you'll find a collection of villages, each a cluster of single-storey brick or cement-block houses, or a scattering of mud huts with thatched roofs.

In the main street, which probably isn't paved, a shop sells everything from cotton rations to pots and pans. Bicycle repairmen hammer and clang, old men play cards and apple-cheeked children peer curiously at foreigners. If there seem to be a lot of children here, it's because family-planning regulations tend to be enforced less literally in the countryside, where each additional pair of hands has always been considered an insurance policy for parents.

If you're invited into a model home, you'll see a few chairs, a table and beds illuminated by a single overhead light bulb. A radio set is a symbol of affluence. Shared toilet and bathing facilities are the rule. You'll be taken to the local medical centre, manned by a "bare-foot doctor", a paramedic, and to the commune's central hospital. Much of the treatment relies on traditional remedies; medicinal herbs are often grown in the hospital grounds.

The headquarters of the commune is usually a building of some consequence. You will be served tea around a big conference table and told about the organization, goals and successes of the enterprise. You'll be taken on a tour of fields and orchards, a new irrigation project, perhaps, or the commune's own factories and workshops. With luck you'll be invited to lunch; an elaborate feast will be laid on in your honour.

Life on a commune may sometimes be harsh, the work back-breaking and the hours long, but increased mechanization has eased the burden of the peasant. Bureaucratic constraints have been relaxed and grass-roots initiative is rewarded. Peasants with imagination and energy can earn money—sometimes small fortunes—in the free markets of nearby villages and towns, selling surplus produce and the yield of their private plots. The official policy of a responsibility system and a contract system now smiles on the enthusiastic peasants who "get rich first"—implying that everyone else will follow in due course.

THE ARTS

Following are a few background notes to help you appreciate the beauty and diversity of Chinese art.

Bronzes. In most other countries Bronze Age artisans concentrated on the production of tools and weapons. Not so in China. Craftsmen here turned bronze-casting into a brilliant art. The ritual goblets, basins and wine vessels of the Shang Dynasty, in use more than 3,000 years ago, have long been esteemed for their technical and aesthetic perfection.

To create a bronze, early Chinese craftsmen constructed a model in wax, coated it with clay and fired it in a kiln. The wax melted and the clay hardened, forming a mould into which the molten bronze could be poured. Typically, Shang bronzes were cast in sections and soldered together.

The designs embellishing these pieces include geometric motifs, figures of animals and demons, and representations of the human face. Then writing was added, making Shang bronzes some of the world's earliest historical documents.

Calligraphy. Fine handwriting is a major art form in China, where literacy was traditionally a sacred or at least scholarly prerogative. A calligrapher uses the same tools and techniques as a painter. He chooses his brush, ink

Masters of every medium, the Chinese excel at bronzework, porcelain and the art of calligraphy.

and paper with care, then stands over an empty scroll imagining how the text of a poem or quotation can best be arranged on the available space. Emotion and elegance go into the brush strokes of each character, whether written in precise classical form or in a running style that looks deceptively spontaneous.

The calligraphic, as well as poetic, achievements of Mao Zedong were highly regarded. His slogans, in reproductions of his own handwriting, were visible everywhere, and the logo of China's biggest newspaper, *The People's Daily,* is still printed as Mao once wrote it.

Ceramics. Since antiquity the Chinese have excelled at the art of the potter, creating a range of useful, yet beautiful, objects: cups and bowls, vases and roof tiles. Tang-Dynasty potters supplied royal tombs with statuettes of soldiers, dancing girls, camels and horses—all of unsurpassed vivacity and colour. Tang craftsmen also perfected the manufacture of porcelain, unknown abroad, exporting it to buyers the world over. The name of the country became synonymous with the product.

In the Song Dynasty, porcelain with an ivory or blueish-white glaze came into vogue, as well as celadon, a translucent pale green glaze, and crackleware, in which the glaze is marked by a network of fine cracks. The Ming Dynasty saw the introduction of the most refined decorations and glazes: cobalt blue was a favourite. But as demand from European buyers soared, Chinese ceramists were induced to copy Western designs, including coats-of-arms, hunting scenes, pictures of ships and so on. The polychrome enamelware of the 18th century (Qing Dynasty) was the last of the great innovations.

Jade. Considering that jade is nearly as hard as diamond, carving it at all is something of an achievement. Fashioning exquisite jade objects—from the burial suits of the Han Dynasty to the screens, wine jars and vases of the Qing—has been the special triumph of the Chinese over the centuries. Ideally, the artist decides what to make of the stone at hand depending on the size, shape and texture.

Modern craftsmen reproduce all the intricacies of classical designs. They also turn out an endless stream of bracelets, pendants and rings. The Chinese believe jade has mystic powers, or at the very least brings good luck. Green jade is the best known variety, but the stone—actually the name "jade" encompasses jadeite and nephrite—can be bright yellow, ruby red or creamy white.

Painting. Countless bronzes, as well as the sculpture and ceramics of ancient Chinese masters, have come down to us intact. But relatively few early paintings have survived the centuries. Some famous works are known only through written descriptions or copies made at a much later date.

The tenets of Chinese painting, expounded in the 6th century A.D., are considered valid today. They demand rhythm and movement, natural proportions, appropriate colours and consistent composition. The Chinese painter doesn't set up an easel and attempt to portray the scene before him; with paper or silk spread upon a table, he works from memory and imagination.

Many Western visitors are perplexed by Chinese painting, with its shifting perspective and lack of fixed viewpoint. Artists never "finish" a painting; works are rolled up and viewed in segments, rather than as a whole. Subjects usually have some redeeming moral value. They also contain references to the work of past masters.

Landscapes dominate Chinese painting, especially the classical style developed in the Song Dynasty: the realism and grandeur of the court artists, the romanticism of the scholars who painted those misty craggy mountains, usually in black and white. During the Yuan era, lengthy poems and inscriptions were added to scenes; Ming artists carried on in the classical manner but showed new interest in bird and flower subjects.

Sculpture. The Han Dynasty brought the earliest monumental sculpture in stone, and relief carving was practised all over China. Confucian rites and ceremonies led to the creation of ancient visions in stone — representations of animals and mythological beasts, and strikingly lifelike portrait statues.

But the inspiration for China's highest achievements in sculpture, such as the glories of the Tang Dynasty more than 1,000 years ago, was Buddhism. Because Buddhism was imported, sculptors were strongly influenced by foreign forms. Some works reflect Indian tastes, or, via India, ancient Greek traditions; others adapt Persian models. Cave temples and shrines preserve remarkable figures of Buddha and attendant disciples notable for their fluid line and compelling rhythm.

Lacquer. Since the feudal Zhou Dynasty, perhaps 2,500 years ago, making works of art from lacquer (a resinous varnish) has been a Chinese speciality. A particular kind of lacquer and colouring agents are required, but most of all it takes time to construct layer upon layer of this fragile substance. Sometimes each of the carefully polished layers is of a different colour, and the finished object is carved to reveal contrast-

49

ing shades—a Song innovation. Or the lustrous surface may be painted or inlaid with mother-of-pearl, like so many sumptuous Tang pieces. Lacquer decorates boxes, fans, trays, even musical instruments, furniture and the pillars of temples and palaces. Still copied today are the elaborate Ming and Qing pieces—intricately carved and coloured a rich red.

Architecture. Before the construction of a building was undertaken, the advice of a geomancer would be solicited. He determined the proper combination of natural and artificial influences on the site, the *feng shui* (literally "wind and water"). This is why palaces and pavilions face south, and why gateways form a maze—to bar evil spirits from the premises. (The high thresholds of traditional Chinese buildings had a more practical secondary function: they kept out flood water and rats.)

Boundary walls are a significant feature of Chinese architecture—encompassing whole cities or small religious or secular compounds. (Carrying the idea to its ultimate extravagance, the Great Wall spanned the entire northern frontier of the country.)

The Chinese constructed mainly in wood, rather than brick or stone. Buildings, rarely more than one storey high, are grouped around quadrangular courtyards. They stand on platforms reached by flights of stairs. Imperial buildings are faced in marble and provided with a ceremonial staircase, generally of carved marble, up

A host of dragons, demons and serpents decorate the pagodas and palaces of Beijing's Forbidden City.

and down which the emperor was carried. Pillars support the roof; the walls merely keep out the wind and rain. Often the supporting wooden pillars and beams are gaudily painted and carved. Even the tallest ancient temples were built without nails; instead, the mortise-and-bracket system was used, in which a projecting piece of wood, the mortise, is fitted securely into a socket or tenon.

Tiles accentuate the curvature of the roof-line, graced with upturned eaves. Sculptures of dragons or other grotesque figures, sometimes strikingly similar to the gargoyles on medieval European churches, are the standard decoration. Woodwork often bears carved or perforated decoration, and ceilings and floors are lavishly inlaid.

The skyline of many a Chinese

town is enhanced by a pagoda. This tower is the Chinese counterpart of the ancient Indian stupa, a domed edifice built to house Buddhist religious relics. Constructed of stone, brick, or less permanently of wood, most pagodas have an octagonal or square plan. They may be anywhere from three to 17 storeys tall—but always an odd number, for superstition's sake.

Gardens. A Chinese garden is a distillation of an idealized landscape, designed to reflect the majesty of nature and to create a feeling of peace. Like ancient landscape scrolls, Chinese gardens are designed to be viewed a little at a time. Surprises are part of the plan; so you never know what to expect round the next corner.

The eye is drawn to tranquil ponds and miniature trees, to artificial hills and grottoes. Ideally, mountains or forests serve as a backdrop. And to add a human element there are pavilions and bridges which zigzag to foil evil spirits. Mystically arranged rockeries figure prominently, too—another reminder that it's all the result of human taste and intervention.

For emperors of the Song Dynasty, West Lake in Hangzhou was an imperial retreat, a place to ponder the problems of state.

WHERE TO GO

The 33 most-visited cities and sights in China, described in detail in this gazetteer, are arranged in alphabetical order. This conveniently puts the capital of the nation in first place. The names of the cities are given in the new Pinyin spelling. For clarity's sake, we also give the spelling by which they have traditionally been known, e.g., Beijing (Peking). The authentic Chinese is provided by the characters, printed alongside.

At the end of the extended gazetteer, you'll find information in brief on an additional 28 cities which, although open to foreign tourists, figure much less frequently on tours.

Choosing an itinerary can be a difficult task, for China is too big to be attempted in any reasonable amount of time. But even a day trip from Hong Kong is better than not seeing China at all. An excessively hasty week might take in Beijing, the Ming Tombs and the Great Wall; the archaeological marvels of Xi'an; the romantic scenery of Guilin; and a glimpse of bustling Shanghai or Guangzhou (Canton). This sort of trip—though you leap around farther and more often than convenient or economical—does have the virtue of touching on the really top-priority attractions.

Less taxing would be a week in and around Shanghai, emphasiz-

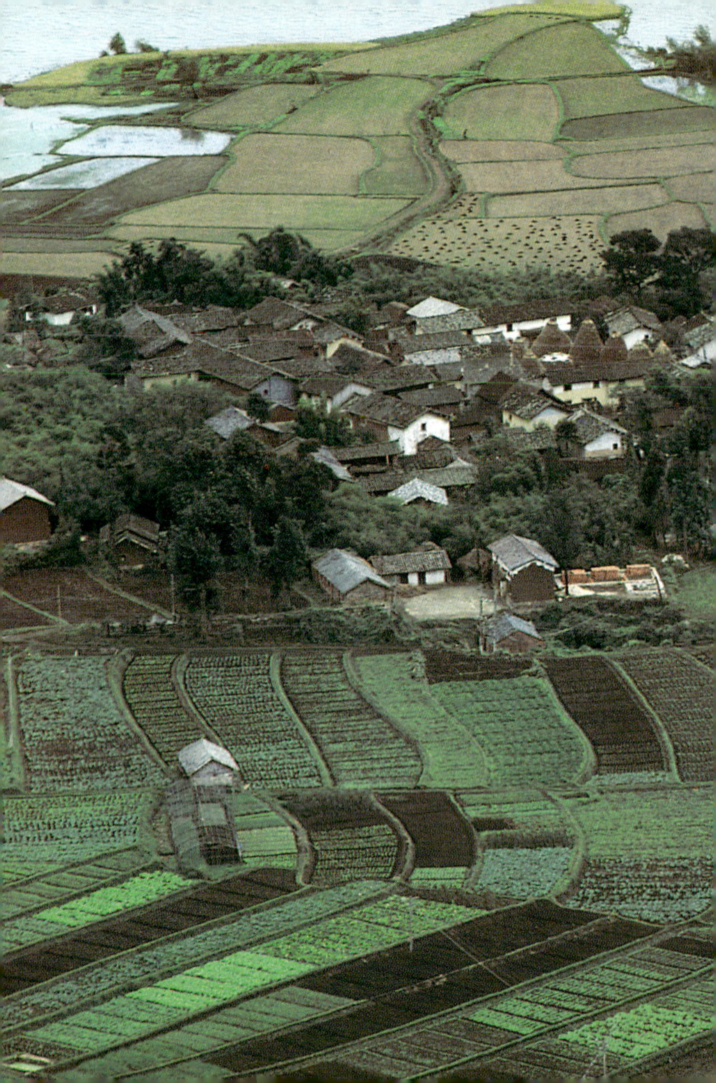

ing the legendary charms of Wuxi, Suzhou and Hangzhou—all three towns on the Grand Canal—with pleasant cruise possibilities.

If you penetrate as far inland as Chongqing, you can take the celebrated three-day boat trip through the Yangtze River Gorges to Wuhan. From there, you could fly to Beijing, Shanghai or Guangzhou for sightseeing, shopping and gourmandizing.

Silk Road enthusiasts fly from Beijing or Xi'an to Urumqi in the far west, with a side-trip to exotic Turpan, and then work back by train to Dunhuang, with its Buddhist cave treasures, and Lanzhou, finally flying on to Beijing or Shanghai. Incidentally, the train-and-bus odyssey from Urumqi to Dunhuang takes 18 hours.

If you want to stay close to Beijing, the better part of a varied week could profitably be spent investigating the ancient carvings of the caves near Datong, and visiting Hohhot, with its Mongolian colour, and Chengde, with its Chinese and Tibetan temples.

Neat fields and newly planted woodlands enclose a picturesque village in Yunnan Province.

55

Clearly, two one-week segments can be neatly combined for a fortnight's touring. But inevitably the most popular itineraries include Beijing, Xi'an and Guilin. Even if you're in a great rush, each place is worth a busy two days at the desperate minimum.

This baby travels in style in a bamboo pram.

BEIJING 北京
(Peking)

A visit to the medieval and modern capital of China is an exhausting but rewarding round of palaces and museums, temples and monuments, factories and stores—a jolting juxtaposition of imperial pomp and contemporary energy.

Beijing has a population of over 9 million, but it's thinly

spread: the city's area is calculated at a staggering 16,800 square kilometres (6,500-odd square miles). For mile after mile, streets are lined with one- and two-storey houses opening onto quiet lanes, where life has changed little since the days of the Qing Dynasty. Around the corner from these cosy alleys are big new housing projects, office buildings, schools and seething markets the trappings of a metropolis in the throes of modernization.

Mostly the city is flat, which is a mercy for the millions who cycle to work in the world's most unlikely rush hour, a chaos of buses and trucks and more bikes than you've seen in your whole life. In the Middle Ages, the emperors decided to do something about the capital's unrelieved flatness. They ordered hills artificially constructed just north of the Forbidden City so they could go up and, in total privacy, enjoy a summer breeze and a bird's-eye view over the curved tile roofs of their imperial compound. Try it yourself, perhaps at dawn, when a thin haze drapes itself over the pavilions, redefining yet softening the features of this story-book skyline. You'll see why the emperors wanted it all for themselves.

A Helping Word

To help you find your way to tourist sites, here are some words (with their Pinyin spelling) to look for:

art gallery	*měi shù guǎn*	美术馆
cave	*dòng, yán, shíku*	洞、岩、石窟
gardens	*huāyuán*	花园
memorial (hall)	*jìniànguǎn*	纪念馆
monastery (Buddhist)	*fósì*	寺
mosque	*qīngzhēnsì*	清真寺
museum	*bówùguǎn*	博物馆
palace	*gōngdiàn*	宫殿
park	*gōngyuán*	公园
temple	*sì, miào*	寺、甪
tomb	*mù*	墓
tower	*tǎ*	塔
zoo	*dòngwùyuán*	动物园

Beijing in History

Not far from the present-day suburbs of Beijing was the habitat of Peking Man, the startling anthropological discovery of the 1920s. A cave near the town of Zhoukoudian revealed the skull of a small-brained but upright ancestor of mankind who lived half a million years ago. Scientists are still sifting the bones.

In spite of this early proof that the Beijing area was inhabited, the place made little stir in the world until the Warring States period (5th to 3rd centuries B.C.) when, known as Jicheng, it became the capital of the Kingdom of Yan. Renamed Yanjing, the town served as capital for the Liao Dynasty in the 10th century A.D. The Jin (Chin) Dynasty of the 12th century called it Zhongdu (Central Capital) and built an imperial palace as well as the Lugou Bridge. (Known abroad as the Marco Polo Bridge, it is still in use.)

Genghis Khan's Mongol hordes levelled Zhongdu in the 13th century, then rebuilt it under the name Dadu (Great Capital). By the time Marco Polo arrived, the city outshone the capitals of Europe.

The Ming Dynasty transferred most of the imperial pomp south to Nanjing in the 14th century. Predictably, Dadu got yet another name, Beiping (Northern Peace), but had to wait more than

50 years to win back its imperial status, and a fresh name. This one—Beijing (Northern Capital)—is still around. So, happily, are the Ming palaces and temples.

At the beginning of the Qing Dynasty, Beijing prospered. New palaces and gardens were laid out, and scholarship flourished. But during the Boxer Rebellion (1900), foreign armies, in retaliation for the siege of their embassies, wrought havoc in the city. This was only the first of many crises which were to rock Beijing: the fall of the empire, the foundation of the Chinese Republic, two world wars, civil war. In 1949 Beijing became the capital of the new People's Republic of China.

Sightseeing

The historic heart of Beijing consists of three concentric cities, rectangular and symmetrical, and a fourth, Outer City, to the south. Most of the miles of walls that protected each of the four cities have been lost to "progress", but the innermost, Forbidden City, still shelters behind its original crenellated fortifications.

Duck for dinner? The Chinese buy theirs live in the market. Right: Golden lettering on an obelisk in Tian An Men Square praises Heroes of the Revolution.

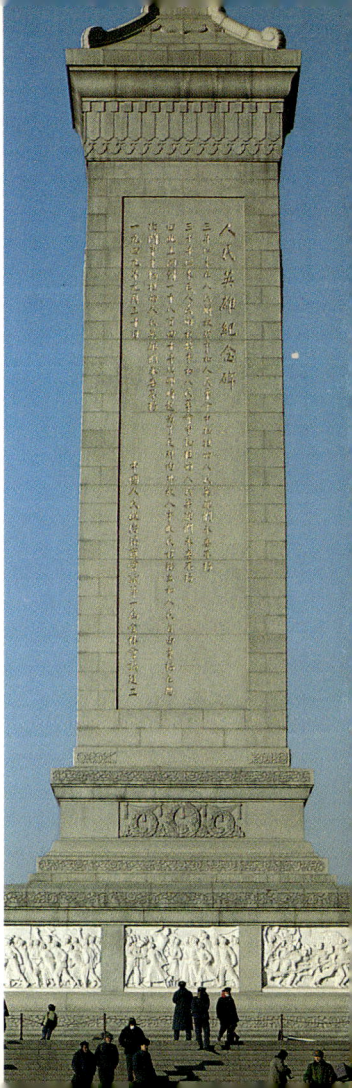

The imperial throne recalls the days when the Son of Heaven held court in this inner pavilion of the Old Palace.

The elegance of this city plan, basically 700 years old, has never been surpassed, though it has been copied in the most improbable places. A precise north-south axis links the main elements, from the Bell Tower all the way to the gate of the Outer City, 8 kilometres (5 miles) to the south. And at the centre of it all is the Forbidden City, imperial heart of the Middle Kingdom.

Tian An Men Square 天安门广场
Called the biggest plaza on earth, Tian An Men Square covers 40 hectares (100 acres) in the very centre of Beijing. Nobody has counted lately, but the square is said to be spacious enough to

opposite side, a facsimile of the handwriting of Zhou Enlai, enlarges on the theme. The importance of the art of calligraphy, clearly, has endured.

The newest building on the square, called the Chairman Mao Zedong Memorial Hall, contains the embalmed body of the man who led the People's Republic for its first 27 years. The **mausoleum**, bigger than Lenin's tomb in Moscow's Red Square, is open on a restricted schedule; tourists may visit by advance arrangement. A grandiose building on the west side of the square, the **Great Hall of the People** (*Renmin Da Hui Tang*), erected in 1959, is the meeting place of the National People's Congress. The banquet hall in the north wing is big enough to seat 5,000 guests.

Far across the plaza, two **museums** in one building cover the history of China and, more specifically, the history of the Chinese revolution. In the former collection are 9,000 items from prehistoric fossils to breathtaking pottery and bronzes; many of China's most glorious archaeological discoveries have been sent here from local museums around the country. Turn left inside the main entrance and go to the bookstall if you want to buy an illustrated brochure in English—most useful if you're on your own, as the explanations on the display cases are in Chinese only.

stage a massive rally of a million people.

Under the emperors the square was only about one-fourth of its present size. In the old, less expansive square Mao Zedong first raised the flag of the new nation on October 1, 1949. A 60-ton granite **obelisk** on the spot has an inscription down one side reproducing Mao's own handwriting: "Eternal glory to the people's heroes." The inscription on the

For many visitors the salient feature of Tian An Men Square is the very vastness of the place, along with the diversity of tourists getting in the way of each other's cameras: Europeans speaking many tongues, Africans, Asians, and colourfully costumed travellers from far corners of China itself. While you're at it you can buy and fly a kite.

Continue to the north side of the square and Tian An Men itself, the **Gate of Heavenly Peace,** leading to the Imperial City. Atop the formidable stone wall is a rostrum for reviewing parades, behind it a massive wooden gate-tower with a double roof. The original 15th-century gate complex was rebuilt in 1651; the big red slogans are more recent, celebrating the People's Republic and unity of the peoples of the world. Above the central portal, through which only the emperor was allowed to pass, hangs a large portrait of the late Chairman Mao.

Forbidden City 紫禁城 (Gu Gong)

Beijing is too sprawling a town for strolling around, so you can forget the sort of charming browse that some historical European cities offer. One exception, though, is the Forbidden City. Here are more than 72 hectares (175 acres) of grandeur: palaces, pavilions, courtyards and gardens, all walled in as a rectangular island within a moat wide enough for naval engagements.

The Forbidden City, so described because it was off-limits to ordinary people for nearly 500 years, is now called the Palace Museum, or the Imperial Palace, or the Ancient Palace. It was designed to contain the auspicious number of 9,999 rooms. You could get lost.

Tourists normally enter the Forbidden City from the south, after a long walk along a cobbled roadway from Tian An Men. The main gate to the compound, **Meridian Gate** *(Wu Men)*, was designed, in the 15th century and in subsequent restorations, to overawe, and even today no one could approach it lightly.

Beyond this powerful defence line stands China's supreme ensemble of ancient architecture. But first another ceremonial gate must be penetrated. The **Gate of Supreme Harmony** *(Tai He Men)* is more modest than the main Meridian Gate, but by any other standards it is most imposing. A pair of monumental bronze lions stand guard.

Next comes the **Hall of Supreme Harmony** *(Tai He Dian)*,

A glimpse into the palaces and gardens of the Forbidden City, "laid out like a chessboard", as Marco Polo described it. Ordinary people were refused entry to this royal enclave.

the biggest building in the Forbidden City and one of China's most beautiful wooden structures. For hundreds of years during the Ming and Qing dynasties this was the tallest building in all Beijing; by law no house could rise higher. (Counting the hall's upswept roof decorations, that meant the limit was about 37½ metres or 123 feet.) Inside, on a raised platform, the "Son of Heaven" sat on his Dragon Throne surrounded by symbols of longevity and power and cowering acolytes, all covered in a fog of incense. To the tune of gongs and chimes, visitors knelt to kowtow nine times.

Much less formal occasions took place in the **Hall of Complete Harmony** *(Zhong He Dian)* behind the Hall of Supreme Harmony. A third hall in this series, the **Hall of Preserving Harmony** *(Bao He Dian)*, was used, among other things, for the palace examinations—essentially the world's first civil service exams. Behind this hall, in the centre of a stairway, is a **ramp** full of sculptured dragons, carved from a single slab of marble weighing more than 200 tons. It was, of course, reserved for the emperor's sedan chair. Thousands of labourers bent their backs to pull the block to this site from the quarry 48 kilometres (30 miles) away; ingeniously, the operation was scheduled for deepest winter so that the load could be slid along specially iced roads.

From here northwards the density of structures in the Forbidden City increases markedly. Many of the old palaces and halls are now used to display the art works and more prosaic belongings of the emperors. Tourists even have a chance to peek through the windows of the concubines' apartments, adding a little spice to the history lesson.

West of all the palaces and pomp is an amusement park for children—a fine spot for people-watching. Most popular is a mad merry-go-round on which the young clients are offered a choice of traditional wooden horses or model cars, motorbikes, or even a horse-drawn sleigh.

Two Parks

Just north of the Imperial Palace complex, along the main imperial axis, is **Jing Shan Park**, better known as Coal Hill *(Mei Shan)*. (The name recalls the fact that the emperors once hoarded coal here; or it may derive from a simple play on words.) The highest point of old Beijing, the hill was created from the earth excavated to form the moat system around the Forbidden City. Each of the five artificial peaks was provided with a romantically designed pavilion. The three-storey **Pavilion of Ten Thousand Springs** *(Wan Chun Ting)*, on the middle peak, offers an inspiring view over the glistening rooftops of the Imperial City, with the modern capital beyond.

Bei Hai Park, Beijing's favourite park, has been a beauty spot for many hundreds of years. Its lake, which young couples now explore in rented rowing boats,

Making a clean sweep of China's city streets.

was created in the 12th century. The graceful **Bridge of Eternal Peace** *(Yong An Qiao)* leads to an artificial island a mile in circumference. On a hill in the centre of the isle stands a Tibetan-style tower, the **White Dagoba** *(Bai Ta)*. In springtime the dagoba seems to burst from waves of green leaves.

A landmark on the north shore of the lake is the Ming Dynasty

The Last of the Ming

It was in a garden fragrant with spring blossom and resonant with the song of birds that the final tragic episode in the history of the Ming Dynasty was played out. After nearly 300 years of Ming rule, Manchu armies were bursting through the Great Wall and the empire was collapsing under the weight of feckless government and internal rebellion.

Meanwhile, a peasant leader took advantage of the disorder to descend on Beijing with a rebel army. In the doomed capital, the court waited powerless for the end.

On March 17, 1644, the Emperor Chong Zhen summoned his family in the old palace, embraced them and ordered his three sons to escape. The empress retired, weeping, to hang herself.

Then, lamenting bitterly that he was fated to preside over the ruin of the dynasty, the emperor wandered through the palace grounds and up into the gardens on Coal Hill. At the entrance to one of the pavilions, he took off his shoes and jewelled imperial headdress and hanged himself from a beam in the doorway.

The rebel triumph was short-lived. The invading Manchus in turn captured Beijing and established the Qing Dynasty which was to reign until the end of all imperial rule in 1911.

Nine Dragon Wall *(Jiu Long Bi)*, decorated with a sweeping scene of dragons playing with giant pearls in a tumultuous sea, all done with glazed tiles to create a dynamic effect.

Temple of Heaven 天坛

Tian Tan Park, known to foreigners as Temple of Heaven Park, is the biggest of Beijing's parks, celebrated for its assembly of thrilling 15th-century architecture.

The highlight is the circular, blue-tile-roofed **Hall of Prayer for Good Harvest** *(Qi Nian Dian)*. This marvel of geometry, art and engineering, built without a single nail, measures 37½ metres (123 feet) to the gilded orb on its topmost roof. In 1889 the masterpiece was struck by lightning and almost burned to the ground. Fortunately, the ruin was quickly restored to its original, resplendent state.

The emperor was carried here in a solemn procession in the first lunar month of each year to pray for a bountiful harvest. The floor plan of the hall provides the key to the building's function: the four central columns represent the seasons; then come two concentric rings of 12 columns each, representing the months and the dozen two-hour periods into which the day was divided; and a total of 28 hardwood pillars symbolize the constellations.

More Historic Sights

Beijing's 17th-century **Lamasery,** the Palace of Harmony and Peace (*Yong He Gong*), was originally the palace of the prince who became the Emperor Yongzheng. The stately complex of wooden buildings, containing nearly one thousand rooms, has been painstakingly restored. The temple recalls 18th-century efforts towards political unity between China, Mongolia and Tibet.

The ancient Beijing **Observatory** was originally part of the city wall. The roof of the castle-like structure is a veritable garden of ancient sundials, sextants and other complex instruments. What look like extra stars in a 17th-century bronze celestial globe turn out to be Japanese bulletholes of World War II vintage.

Beijing Zoo

China's largest zoo, in the northwestern sector of Beijing, features on many tourist itineraries. Best known for its lovable giant pandas, it also houses other unusual species from various parts of the country—Manchurian tigers, Tibetan yaks, snow leopards, and the weird Père David's deer, known to the Chinese as the "quadruple unlikeness" (*Si bu xiang*) because it has the characteristics of the deer, the reindeer, the ox and the donkey. Local children come to stare at the imported beasts.

Summer Palace 颐和园

The Chinese name for this convergence of natural and manmade beauty is Yi He Yuan—the Park of Nurtured Harmony. Foreigners call the whole 280 hectares (700 acres) the Summer Palace. Actually, the palaces, pavilions, temples and halls occupy only a small part of the dreamily landscaped area. By far the largest feature of the park is **Kunming Lake.**

Contemporary Chinese historians wax indignant that, under the Qing Dynasty, funds appropriated for the imperial navy were siphoned off to make Yi He Yuan an ever more luxurious private park. Among the items on which the Empress Dowager Ci Xi squandered the naval budget is an astonishing, double-decker **Marble Boat** beached at the edge of the lake. It's the kind of folly only the most unselfconscious potentate could undertake—mad ness but ever so charming.

Among the outstanding structures in the park: the **Hall of Joyful Longevity** (*Le Shou Tang*), the **Seventeen-Arch Bridge,** and a wooden **gallery** 728 metres (nearly half a mile) long. This covered way, interrupted by octagonal pavilions, is decorated with landscape paintings and depictions of Chinese legends; many were damaged during the Cultural Revolution. (Nowadays, Chinese vandals tend to scribble graffiti on the walls. The ones who sign their names and home towns — the most common inscriptions — are tracked down and fined.)

🚶 **The Great Wall** 万里长城

It's about 80 kilometres (50 miles) from the centre of Beijing northwest to the most visited stretch of the Great Wall of China, at Badaling Pass. The trip telescopes history, from the modern capital through outskirts where donkey carts and cargo-carrying bicycles share the road, past farms where nothing seems to have changed for centuries, to a harsh mountain range where nearly a million workers walled in an empire. Like all the real wonders of the world, this one is more awesome at first hand than in any film or book.

The first elements of the wall system were built more than 2,000 years ago, but the most ambitious expansion and consolidation of (about 6,000 kilometres or 3,700 miles). It remains the only man-made landmark visible to the naked eye from the moon.

The restored section of the wall at Badaling Pass, undulating up the unexpectedly steep hillsides, can be a test of a tourist's endurance. Everyone is out of breath, exchanging sympathetic smiles along the way as they ascend to one or another of the crenellated towers. If you kept walking west you would wind up at the edge of the Gobi Desert.

As if proving the point, a two-humped camel is stationed here, available for souvenir photos at 10 yuan a snap. The stalls near the car park sell diplomas certifying that the holder has indeed climbed the Great Wall. Don't forget your walking shoes.

The Ming Tombs 十三陵

On the way to the Great Wall is the peaceful valley the Ming emperors chose as their burial ground. The two attractions are usually combined in a single excursion.

In 1407 the Emperor Yong Le ordered a search for a suitable burial place with auspicious "wind and water" conditions, as well as appropriate grandeur. This site proved so perfect that all but three of the succeeding Ming rulers were entombed in the same valley.

The **Sacred Way** to the tombs

A monument to folly and extravagance, the Marble Boat of Empress Ci Xi dwarfs pleasure craft on the lake at the Summer Palace.

the project began under the Ming Dynasty in the 14th century. And so the serpentine stone bulwark and elevated highway became Wan Li Chang Cheng—"The Wall Ten Thousand Li Long"

begins at a great marble gateway more than four centuries old. Beyond this is the main gate with three archways; the middle passage was used only once in each reign—for the delivery of the emperor's remains to his tomb. Then comes the **Avenue of the Animals,** lined with massive statues of real and mythical beasts, standing and kneeling.

The largest and, of course, oldest tomb belonged to Yong Le himself. Called **Chang Ling,** this tomb is sumptuous indeed. For instance, the **Hall of Eminent Favours** (*Ling En Dian*) is among

Animals, warriors and mandarins of stone guard the Sacred Way along which Ming emperors were carried to their tombs.

the largest wooden buildings in China. Each of the 32 gilded pillars supporting the coffered ceiling is made from the wood of a huge tree from south-west China; it took more than five years to ship the timber here.

Ninety-one steps take you down below ground level to the entrance to **Ding Ling** (the tomb of the Emperor Wan Li, whose reign lasted nearly 50 years from 1573 to 1620). It took 30,000 workers six years to build this underground palace. Most of the regalia and artefacts on show, including the red wooden coffin-containers in the burial vault, are copies of the items discovered during excavations in the 1950s. Some of the original crowns, jewels and ornate hairpins and combs are on display in the nearby museum buildings.

CHANGSHA 长沙

If you happen to go to Changsha by train, you will arrive at the second biggest railway station in China, a distinction quite out of proportion to the amount of rail traffic or the size of the city. The explanation is to be found in recent history: until the late 1970s, legions of pilgrims converged on this provincial capital in search of the roots of Chairman Mao Zedong.

Now that Mao's cult has been set aside, the stations and the shrines are uncrowded and Changsha has returned to its age-old role as a rather prosaic regional centre of trade and culture. But the fertile countryside is attractive, the handicrafts are outstanding, and archaeology enthusiasts can look forward to stunning revelations.

The capital of Hunan Province, Changsha lies along the Xiang River, a wide and often turbulent stream that empties into the Yangtze. The long thin strip of **Orange Island** *(Juzi Zhou)*, rich in oranges, among other crops, bisects the river. (The name of the city derives from the appearance of the island; Changsha means a long sand-bar.) From the pavilion at the southern tip there is an engrossing view of sampans, barge trains and passenger ships.

On the far side of the river, fragrant forests climb the slopes of **Yue Lu Hill,** a favourite escape

from the subtropical heat of the city in summer. One of the evergreen trees in the mountainside Lu Shan Temple is more than 1,700 years old.

For most tourists the prime attraction of the region is in the north-east part of town: the **Hunan Provincial Museum,** with its renowned relics of the Han Dynasty. Here is gripping evidence that Chinese royalty, at least, lived a most refined life in the time of the Han emperors. On show are silks, ceramics and lacquerware of unbelievable sophistication, and alluring figurines and musical instruments.

All these artefacts and works of art survived to this day because they were buried in coffins within coffins in subterranean royal tombs. A grotesque exhibit which never fails to draw crowds is the well-preserved corpse of what is thought to be the wife of a royal personage. She still has hair on her head and, you might imagine, a 2,000-year-old scream on her lips.

The deceased was discovered, wrapped in many layers of silk and linen, in one of three tombs unearthed at a place called **Mawangdui,** about 4 kilometres (2½ miles) east of the museum. You can go to the site and walk atop the gentle hills that concealed these treasures. It all came to light in 1972 when workers were digging an air-raid shelter.

Hunan's **First Teachers' Training School** *(Di Yi Shi Fan)*, which was burned down in 1938, was reconstructed in 1968 in its original form—resembling a European monastery, with arcades and gardens. During the Cultural Revolution visitors thronged the institution every day, for this is where Mao Zedong studied and taught for a total of seven years. They have reproduced the classroom of 30 desks where he sat

The Chinese have been embroidering silk for 3,000 years.

and the crowded dormitory where he slept under a mosquito net.

During the early 1970s, millions of excursionists went to the village of **Shaoshan,** Mao's birthplace, two hours from Changsha by tour bus. The principal sights are the house where he was born, quite roomy by local standards, and a museum with all the exhibits in duplicate, filling two mirror-image wings designed to double the crowd capacity.

Tourists in Changsha are taken on tours of the local **embroidery factory,** where Hunan's 2,000-year handicraft tradition flourishes. Fully 80 per cent of the unit's output of decorative embroidery is exported—mostly to Japan, the United States and Australia. Staff artists paint original designs, usually of landscapes, animals, birds or flowers, which the artisans (all women) reproduce stitch by microscopic stitch in colourful silk. The proudest product here is double-faced embroidery with a different picture on each side. Each piece sells for thousands of yuan.

The Hunan **porcelain factory** is also something of a tourist attraction. Its high-powered production lines are manned by 2,500 employees; about 20 million cups, saucers and plates are exported each year. A small shop on the premises sells figurines, teacups, pitchers and vases.

Changsha is the place to try the spicy cuisine of Hunan Province. Like the better known recipes of neighbouring Sichuan (Szechuan) Province, hot chilli peppers come to the fore. In recent years Hunan-style restaurants have sprung up in the big cities of Europe and America, to acclaim from connoisseurs.

CHENGDE 承德

In summer the trip to Chengde (formerly Jehol), about 250 kilometres (150 miles) north-east of Beijing, may well be the prettiest train ride anywhere in China. Fertile fields alternate with stony hills miraculously sprouting trees and wild flowers. In the hamlets along the way, trim houses are roofed with thatch or traditional tile with winged projections.

After five hours on a train, some tourists are disappointed to find that Chengde looks, at first glance, like any other northern Chinese industrial town. The happy difference is that the dreariness is interspersed with beautifully sited old monasteries and an imperial pleasure-ground big enough to be protected by a wall 10 kilometres (6 miles) long.

The palace and gardens of Chengde, in Hebei (Hopei) Province, provided summertime escape for the emperors of the Qing Dynasty. Its altitude—about 350 metres (more than 1,100 feet) above sea level—relieves the heat, as do the surrounding mountains, forests and rivers.

Chengde **Mountain Resort** (*Bi Shu Shan Zhuang*), in the northern part of the city, begins at the ceremonial Li Zheng Gate,

China's landscapes are an eternal source of inspiration.

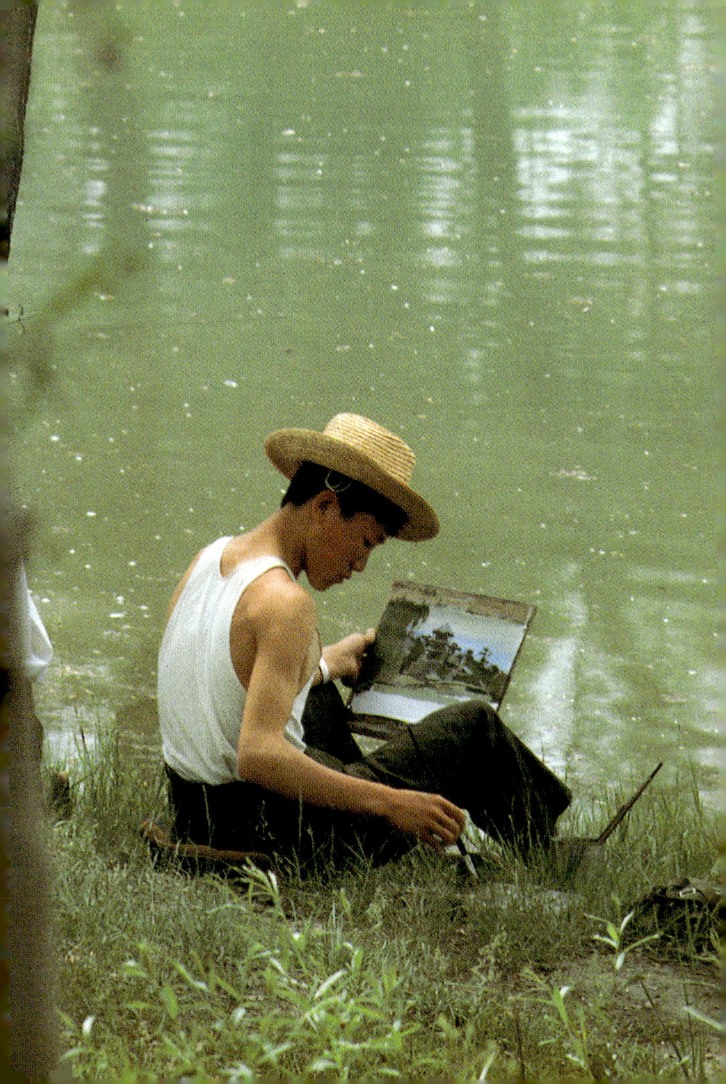

flanked by two marble lions. The pavilions within the palace compound now serve as a small museum. Among the exhibits: bows and arrows and Chinese flintlocks, rare jade and porcelain, and the sedan chairs in which the emperors were transported all the way from Beijing.

The halls and courtyards are eminently regal, yet they inspire a feeling of relaxation appropriate to the setting. The plain wooden corridors connecting the buildings contrast with the illustrated passageways of Beijing's Summer Palace.

The landscape beyond the palace features many of the romantic elements of Chinese tradition—a lake and lotus ponds, forests, causeways and bridges, pavilions, towers and a pagoda. The **House of Mists and Rains** (Yan Yu Lou), a two-storey tower in South China style, is one of the buildings alongside the lake. From here, on a misty day, the emperor could enjoy a scene resembling an old Chinese painting. Today tourists can cross the lake in a hand-poled ferryboat, or rent rowing boats and drift at their own pace.

Just north of the lake, in the **Park of Ten Thousand Trees** (Wan Shu Yuan), the emperor gave an audience to the first British ambassador, Lord Macartney, in 1793. The peaceful setting failed to dispel mutual misunderstandings.

Beyond the wall surrounding the palace and its gardens, exotic roofs of the **Eight Outer Temples,** as they are known, rise on the surrounding hillsides. Among the highlights: the **Temple of Universal Peace** (Pu Ning Si) displays features of Han architecture; but suddenly, up a flight of stone steps and through a low gate, you are transported to Tibet—or at least to a replica of the Samadhi Temple in Tibet. The grand "Thousand-armed and Thousand-eyed" Goddess of Mercy, Guan Yin, carved of wood, rises more than 22 metres (72 feet). In truth it has but 42 arms and 45 eyes.

More Tibetan reflections beautify the temple called **Xu Mi Fu Shou** (the Chinese translation of the name of the sixth Panchen Lama's headquarters). From the hillside above there is a sumptuous view of the main roof of the temple, embellished by eight gilded copper dragons in furious flight.

The most striking of the Tibetan-style structures of Chengde is the **Pu Tuo Zhong Cheng Temple,** completed in 1771 as an approximate copy of the Potala palace in Lhasa. It's a stiff climb of 164 stairs from the base to the "ground" floor of this six-storey red palace. Inside the seemingly invulnerable brick walls, a wooden temple occupies the centre of the structure.

CHENGDU 成都
(Chengtu)

Balmy, often misty weather keeps Chengdu green and full of flowers the year round. It's the climate in which bamboo thrives. And bamboo is the staple of the giant panda. The best place to see these cuddly-looking beasts is the Chengdu **Zoo,** because it has more of them (about a dozen) than any other zoo in the world. The thin bamboo stalks they find so delicious are grown right in the grounds. Because they are the stars of this important tourist attraction, the pandas are assigned high-ceilinged, spacious cages and outdoor play areas.

Chengdu is the capital of Sichuan (Szechuan) Province, the natural habitat of the giant panda and the most populous province in all China. Sichuan, about the size of France, has a population of more than 100 million. This is not the place to go to escape the crowds.

During the era of the Three Kingdoms, in the 3rd century, Chengdu was the capital of the feudal Kingdom of Shu. The principal monument from that time is the **Temple of Marquis Wu** *(Wu Hou Ci),* a complex of halls and gardens in the southern suburbs, commemorating the kingdom's prime minister. Known in his lifetime (A.D. 181-234) as Zhuge Liang, he was posthumously ennobled for his role in unifying the

---

When the Bamboo Flowers...

The Giant Panda, one of the world's best-loved animals, has been known to science for little more than a hundred years, yet it may vanish before this century is out. For the future of this furry black and white beast is linked with the forests of bamboo that cover the mountains of South-West China, its only home.

The varieties of bamboo on which the panda feeds have a way of suddenly flowering and dying off over vast areas, at intervals of decades, sometimes even a century. It takes many months for the plants to grow again.

Several hundred pandas died of starvation a few years ago when large tracts of bamboo flowered. Soon there may be another bamboo famine; Chinese and Western scientists are working on plans to save the pandas when that happens.

Ten areas have been set aside as panda reserves; a research station is studying the movements and feeding habits of the animal; and Chengdu zoo, which already breeds captive pandas, is geared to provide refuge and food for stricken creatures during a bamboo crisis.

Today, there are thought to be only a thousand giant pandas left in the wild. No one knows how many will survive the next time the bamboo flowers.

region and developing its economy and culture. In the main hall, built in the Tang Dynasty, are gilt statues of the prime minister, his son and grandson; the latter died in battle at the age of 14.

Chengdu's biggest and most renowned religious monument, 28 kilometres (17 miles) north of the city, is the **Divine Light Monastery** *(Bao Guang Si)*. The most photographed element of this vast establishment is the **stupa,** a slightly crooked 13-storey pagoda. It was built, of stone, at the end of the Tang Dynasty, replacing an ancient wooden pagoda on the same spot. The five main halls of the monastery are filled with works of art—Buddhist sculptures, religious and landscape paintings, and examples of many schools of calligraphy. One 19th-century hall contains 500 statues of Buddhist saints, bigger than life-size. The "Ancestor Garden", formerly reserved for retired monks, has been appropriated for the use of foreign tourists only— as a tearoom. (The monastery, which once housed 3,000 monks, now has about 30.)

Chinese literary pilgrims are drawn to the **Thatched Cottage of Du Fu** *(Du Fu Caotang)*—a shrine, museum and park at the spot where a great poet of the Tang Dynasty lived for several

years. Du Fu (hitherto spelled Tu Fu) lived from 712 to 770 and wrote more than 1,400 poems. Some have been published in as many as 15 languages.

Another restful spot is the **River Viewing Pavilion** *(Wang Jiang Lou)*, in a park along the south bank of the Jin (Brocade) River. It's said that more than 100 kinds of bamboo grow in the park, including some imported varieties. As in other traditional Chinese parks, there are pavilions and towers, rock gardens, ponds and shady paths.

River viewing of a different type is recommended at the site of the **Du Jiang Yan Irrigation System,** 57 kilometres (35 miles) north-west of Chengdu. This bold irrigation- and flood-control project, built in the 3rd century B.C., is still in use. The lush hills along the shore provide a poetic setting for an engineering wonder.

In the centre of town some neighbourhoods retain an almost medieval look. Two-storey houses, some sagging with age, line the narrow streets. They have shops on the ground floor and living quarters above, with

Pandas and opera stars top the bill in Sichuan Province.

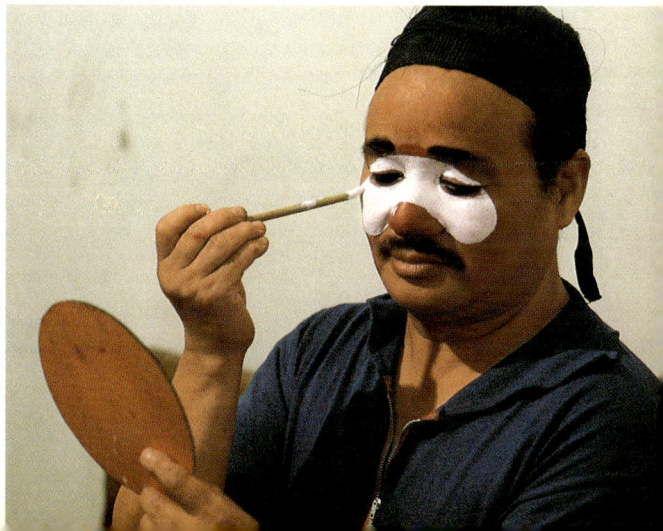

wooden balconies and distinctive carved designs. But "progress" is irresistible. On the site of the ancient viceroy's palace, in the very centre of Chengdu, stands a heavy, columned socialist realist building; a giant statue of Mao Zedong graces the entrance. The edifice is now a department store. In the main hall shoppers are inspired by portraits of Mao, Marx, Engels, Lenin and Stalin. A special department catering to foreign tourists features such local specialities as Shu embroidery, toy pandas (of rabbit fur), pottery and bamboo ware.

By way of local colour, don't turn down a chance to see Szechuan Opera. To make things more challenging, it's all sung in the local dialect; but you can just relax and watch the spectacle of mime, dance and acrobatics.

As for Szechuan cuisine, one of the four great schools of Chinese cooking, it runs to such imaginative heights as "abalone and chrysanthemums", "peonies and butterflies", and "stewed bear's trotters in brown sauce". More homely recipes involve pork, chicken and beancurd, enlivened with chilli peppers, ginger or sweet-and-sour sauce. More informally, Chengdu's streets are well supplied with dumpling and noodle stalls.

Many make Chengdu their starting point for excursions to **Mt. Emei** (see p. 129).

CHONGQING 重庆
(Chungking)

Although the city's history goes back thousands of years, Chongqing was never a cultural centre, and it isn't today. It has no spectacular temples, palaces or archaeological sites. Rather, it is a place to see the daily life of a major Chinese industrial city, as well as the jump-off point for some outstanding excursions.

In the Qin Dynasty, in the 3rd century B.C., the city was the capital of the dreamily named Kingdom of Ba. Its present name—Chongqing means "Double Jubilation"—dates from the Middle Ages, commemorating a lucky streak in the life of the local prince. Until the last few years it was spelled Chungking, by which name the city was best known in the West as the political and military capital of the Nationalist government from 1939 to 1945, the wartime redoubt of Chiang Kai-shek.

Chongqing is the main city of subtropical Sichuan (Szechuan) Province, with a population of more than 6 million. Set on a promontory where the Yangtze and Jialing rivers meet, this starkly industrial city of smokestacks is crucial to transportation and commerce in south-west China.

The sightseeing you remember best may be the lively **free market** lining the hundreds of steps that descend higgledy-piggledy from the hills of central Chongqing to the river. Hustling, bustling peasants hawk the rich harvest of the surrounding farming country—cabbages and oranges, eggs and live chickens (they are weighed while flapping), river fish and squirming eels, and table after table of the most fragrant spices.

The steep stone stairway, which appears not to have been cleaned since the Ming Dynasty, is treacherously overlaid with mud and muck, so wear your safest shoes and walk with care. Happily, at the bottom of the long descent through the market, there is a terminal for the funicular that returns you to the top of the town.

An extraordinary architectural creation, called the **Chongqing People's Hall,** was built in 1953 to serve as a 4,000-seat conference hall plus hotel. It is an attempted compromise between the styles of the Ming and Qing dynasties and the needs of conference delegates in a People's Republic.

Red Crag Village (*Hong Yan Cun*) is the site of a wartime liaison office set up by the Communists, who tried to cooperate with the Nationalists in their joint struggle against the Japanese. Chinese schoolchildren and factory groups are taken on tours of the headquarters, including the room occupied by Zhou Enlai throughout the war.

Also in the domain of political

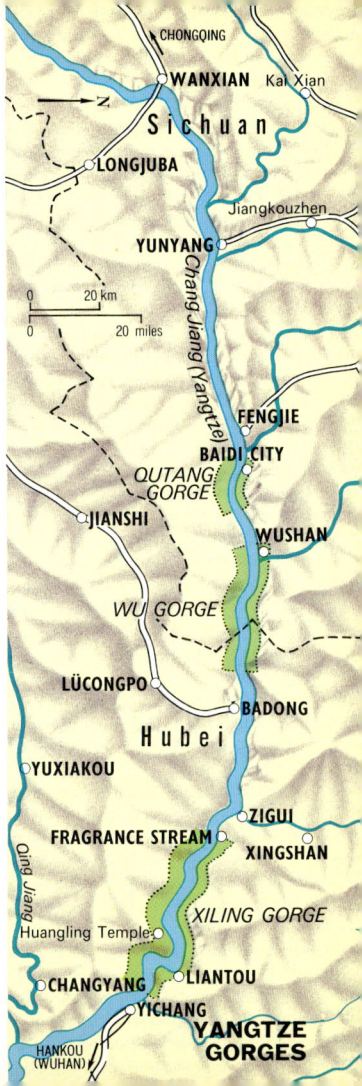

CHONGQING
WANXIAN Kai Xian
Sichuan
LONGJUBA
Jiangkouzhen
YUNYANG
Chang Jiang (Yangtze)
0   20 km
0   20 miles
FENGJIE
BAIDI CITY
QUTANG GORGE
JIANSHI
WUSHAN
WU GORGE
LÜCONGPO
BADONG
Hubei
YUXIAKOU
ZIGUI
FRAGRANCE STREAM
XINGSHAN
Qing Jiang
XILING GORGE
Huangling Temple
CHANGYANG LIANTOU
YICHANG
HANKOU (WUHAN)
YANGTZE GORGES

history, two former Nationalist prisons outside the town are now considered monuments to the Revolutionary cause. The **U.S.- Chiang Kai-shek Criminal Acts Exhibition Hall** — so goes the catchy title — includes cells and torture chambers. Western visitors are not usually taken here unless they specifically request it. This is largely in deference to the sensitivities of Europeans and Americans, who are blamed for collusion with the Nationalists in the excesses of their anti-communist struggle.

Because of Chongqing's notoriously torrid summer weather — it's known as one of the "ovens" of the Yangtze — hills and parks are a welcome refuge. **Loquat Hill** (*Pipa Shan*), the city's high-spot, has gardens, a tearoom and some splendid panoramas. The Northern and Southern **Hot Springs** parks (*Bei Wen Quan* and *Nan Wen Quan*) are also popular gathering places, with well-kept public gardens. A typical Chongqing method of escaping the heat is to take refuge in a cool cave. During the years of Japanese air raids, hundreds of air-raid shelters were dug into the mountains here, and some have been turned into cafés and restaurants.

In Chongqing try to sample the authentic cuisine of Szechuan, preferably in one of the many small restaurants; the hotels catering to tour groups tend to restrict themselves to bland offerings for fear the local hot chilli pepper, essential ingredient of the magnificent Szechuan cooking, will prove too strong for the uninitiated.

Another speciality of this province, the giant panda, may be admired at the outstanding Chongqing **Zoo,** in the southern part of town. The panda pits are outdoors and several of these lumbering teddy-bear characters are usually visible — single-mindedly enjoying their own form of Szechuan cuisine, bamboo.

Yangtze River Cruise
扬子江旅游船

China's most exciting boat trip is the cruise through the Yangtze River Gorges. It takes at least three days from Chongqing to Wuhan, and as many as five days in the reverse direction, bucking the considerable tide. Until very recently the voyage through the famous gorges, known collectively as San Xia (Three Gorges), was an extended, risky adventure. Until only 50 years ago, thousands of coolies towed vessels upstream by means of ropes, and the channel was fraught with hidden obstacles.

The great Yangtze River threads its way through the heart of China.

The most awesome scenery is concentrated between the Sichuan city of Baidi and Nanjin Pass in Hubei Province. The sight of the Yangtze water rushing between the sheer walls and evocative rock formations never fails to stir the traveller's spirit.

The grottoes of Dazu shelter thousands of Buddhist carvings.

Tourists can choose between two itineraries: the three-day voyage downstream aboard a simple Chinese passenger ship, or a five-day trip with shore visits and every luxury on board one of the new chartered cruise ships reserved for foreigners. (The latter can also be taken upstream, starting at Wuhan and also lasting five days.) The normal river boat, which Chinese travellers use, is

divided into second-, third-, fourth- and fifth-class accommodation, first class being mysteriously nonexistent. The chartered ships, with luxury class alone, charge several times more; they are normally reserved for package tours organized abroad, but vacancies may be available at the last moment in the event an excursion is not full. Apply at the CITS office in Chongqing or Wuhan.

Dazu Stone Sculptures
大足石刻

One of China's great artistic wonders, rated on a par with the Mogao Grottoes on the Silk Road in Dunhuang, is the Buddhist sculptural treasure of Dazu. This district, 160 kilometres (100 miles) north-west of Chongqing, was so inaccessible in earlier times that many thousands of statues were never exposed to pillage. It's still a difficult drive, compensated by the richness of the Sichuan scenery.

The stone carvings of Dazu were begun late in the 9th century during the Tang Dynasty; almost all of the work was finished by the end of the Southern Song period 400 years later. Although Buddhism is the central theme, there are also sculptures of historical or human-interest subjects.

Northern Hill *(Bei Shan)*, only a couple of kilometres north of Dazu, begins with a Buddhist temple and a big, animated square. Descending into a wide, rocky valley, you see thousands of sculptures; every inch of stone seems to have been carved. Don't miss "The Wheel of the Universe" in Grotto 136; among the perfectly preserved figures are statues of two holy women, the Bodhisattvas Manjusri and Samatabhadra, who triumphed over evil. Helping to make Northern Hill an overwhelming experience is the presence of Buddhist pilgrims.

Frescoes in Datong's Great Temple of Treasure exalt scenes from the life of Buddha.

Less easily accessible, and no longer an active place of worship, **Treasure Peak** *(Bao Ding Shan)* is nonetheless a moving artistic achievement. The biggest single work, an immense reclining Buddha, is surrounded by the infinitely smaller statues of lifelike disciples. Whereas grotto sculpture in China is usually laid out more or less spontaneously, the caves here were all planned to the last detail before the first stone was chipped, thus eliminating repetition.

Dazu can theoretically be seen in a hectic and exhausting day trip, but the treasures merit more than a hasty glance. A new hotel is being built to supplement the present spartan accommodation.

DATONG 大同
(Tatung)

It takes seven or eight hours to travel by train from Beijing to Datong, in Shanxi (Shansi) Province. Train enthusiasts will enjoy not only the journey but the chance to see many quaint steam locomotives at work in and around Datong, a rail junction in the centre of China's richest coal-mining region. Coal is the logical fuel to pull the long trains transporting the region's coal to the rest of the country. Steam also powers many locomotives hauling general freight, as well as some passenger trains. Datong (metropolitan population 900, 000) is the home of one of the last steam engine factories in the world, a major industry capable of turning out a locomotive every working day. (Group visits to this factory or a coal mine must be organized in advance.)

Sightseeing in Town

Datong itself is a coal-mining and industrial city set on a loess plateau 1,000 metres (3,280 feet) above sea level. The summers are short here on the edge of Inner Mongolia, and winters are glacial. It's not the sort of place poets would eulogize, yet for nearly a century (A.D. 398 to 494) it served as the capital of the Northern Wei Dynasty.

Three monasteries and a famous dragon screen recall Datong's once stately history. The **Nine Dragon Wall** *(Jiu Long Bi)*, a 14th-century Ming landmark, stands in the old part of town among the narrow streets of single-storey houses. This is said to be the largest and oldest screen of its type anywhere in China. The ceramic mural shows nine dragons, each in a different dynamic pose. When the sun reflects on the pool that runs along the base of the wall, the glazed tile figures seem to come to life.

The only monastery still functioning in Datong, the **Upper Hua Yan Monastery,** was built under the Liao Dynasty in the 11th century. Much of the edifice was destroyed in the last years of the Liao but it was reconstructed by the Jin in 1140. The monastery faces east and not, as was customary, south. The main building, the Great Temple of Treasure *(Da Xiong Bao Dian)*, is reckoned to be one of the two biggest Buddhist halls still standing in China. The ceiling is composed of 749 illustrated squares, no two the same. Along the walls are statues of 20 celestial warriors, all with different costumes and complexions.

It's a short walk to the **Lower Hua Yan Monastery,** where the incense smoke of the centuries has made the gold-plated statues look like old bronze. The venerable wooden buildings have survived at least three major earthquakes, thanks to their tenon-and-mortise construction. A souvenir shop at the monastery sells, among other things, rubbings of historic inscriptions.

The vast **Shan Hua Monastery,** facing the old city wall, dates from the Tang Dynasty, but it was largely rebuilt after a fire in the Middle Ages. In the grand, red-walled pavilion stand 24 celestial guardians, each of distinct mien. A circular "moon gate" in the side wall of the monastery leads to the **Five Dragon Wall** *(Wu Long Bi)*, transplanted here from a former Confucian temple. This ceramic screen resembles the lavish Nine Dragon Wall in the town centre, but here the middle dragon, terrifyingly, faces forward.

Yungang Caves 云岗石窟

Most tourists head for Datong in pursuit of history and art. The city is best known as the base for trips to the Yungang Caves (16 km.

[10 miles] west of Datong), which contain China's most treasured legacy of ancient Buddhist sculpture.

When the pious project was undertaken 1,500 years ago, about 100,000 statues were carved into the walls of the rock temples dug into the cliff. About 50,000 statues—from the size of a postage stamp to the height of a five-storey house—remain, in spite of the rigours of time, the weather and marauders.

Visitors enter through a monastery where 2,000 monks once lived. A wooden structure four storeys high, built in the Ming Dynasty, blocks the winds that blast the caves. Carvings of the fanciful Third Son of the Dragon protect the building from fire.

Because restoration work continues on the easternmost caves, tours normally begin at Cave No. 5, containing China's largest **seated Buddha** figure—17 metres (56 feet) high. The gold plating, an afterthought, was added in the Qing Dynasty. As in most of the caves, the walls are filled with niches and small statues.

In Cave No. 6, nearly square in plan, a pagoda reaches to the ceiling. The life of the Buddha from birth to the attainment of nirvana is illustrated in an intricately carved **frieze** running around the pagoda walls and the sides of the cave. The decoration in this cave is considered the supreme achievement of Yungang.

Cave No. 7 is notable for the beautifully carved ceiling. At the entrance to Cave No. 8, graceful, Indian-style statues face each other. Cave No. 9 contains the smallest of all Buddha figures here—2 centimetres. (¾ inch) high. In Cave No. 10 note the Greek influence in the headdress of the guardian figure carved at the entrance.

Cave No. 11 is said to contain some 12,000 **Buddha figures** —more than any other cave. High up on the wall is a tablet reporting that 83 artists worked for six years to complete the carvings in this one grotto. In Cave No. 12, heavenly **musicians** carved over the entrance are playing 12 different ancient instruments. Notice an unusual feature of the giant statue in Cave No. 13: the Buddha's right wrist is supported by the small figure of a four-armed sportsman.

Cave No. 14 has suffered severe damage. (In general the wind has eroded outward-facing walls in most of the caves; the best preserved carvings tend to be on the opposite walls.) The **Cave of Ten Thousand Buddhas** is the name of Cave No. 15; the figures are arranged in a pigeonhole grid pattern.

The oldest caves of the whole complex—dating from the 5th century—are numbered 16 to 20.

(The present east-to-west numbering scheme, inaugurated in modern times, bears little resemblance to the system used in earlier centuries.)

Left: *Paintings like this decorate many a Chinese home.* Right: *Terraced paddy fields climb the hillsides in Gansu Province.*

In Cave No. 16, three holes pierced through the outer wall show the original positions of three Buddhas appropriated by foreign collectors; tour guides here say they are now in New York's Metropolitan Museum. Cave No. 17, like its neighbours on either side, has an oval floorplan. The Buddha's upper arms sport Greek-style armbands.

The giant standing Buddha in

Cave No. 18 wears a strange vestment called the **Thousand Buddha Robe;** on the front of the garment the sculptor has carved a throng of mini-Buddha figures. Cave No. 20, the last one carved while Datong was the capital of the Northern Wei Dynasty, is occupied by a **giant seated Buddha.** It's all the more dramatic since the front wall crumbled away, leaving the statue open to the sky.

DUNHUANG 敦煌
(Tunhuang)

A sleepy, sand-blasted desert town in Gansu Province, Dunhuang could hardly be more difficult to reach—usually 24 hours on a train followed by two or three hours by bus or jeep along a cruelly bumpy road. Even so, modern transport proves more convenient than the Silk Road camel trains that used to stop here.

Seeing the Grottoes

The sign at the entrance to the Mogao Caves lists all the things you must not do. You're not to sit on or lean over the fences, nor may you carry "bags, cameras, straw hats, sticks, etc.". (They worry that such projections might inadvertently scrape against the murals.) Another restriction: "Children under 1.4 metres tall not permitted in caves."

Perhaps the most urgent prohibition refers to flash cameras; the light would shorten the life of the murals. Because of the desert climate and the pigments used in the paintings, the colours have endured. But to protect them, the caves are kept in darkness. Guides illuminate pertinent points with torches (flashlights), thus adding a hint of archaeological adventure to the proceedings.

You'd be wise to carry a pocket torch too for close-up examination of details the guide might have skimmed over—or not noticed at all. Full-colour postcards, slides and picture books, along with artists' copies of cave paintings, are sold at a shop on the premises.

Join a tour if you don't want to lose time skulking around the locked cave entrances waiting for someone to let you in.

Finally, take a sweater or jacket along. Inside the caves it can be very chilly.

Camels still work in and around Dunhuang, pulling ploughs or transporting cargo. If you've just come from over-populated eastern China, you may feel all but alone in a town of only 10,000. Although donkey carts and bicycles occasionally impinge on the tranquillity of the main street, the townsfolk have time to stand around and gossip.

In China even provincial museums can be treasure troves. The **Dunhuang County Museum**, in the centre of the town, overflows with Silk Road relics, from works of art to 2,000-year-old chopsticks.

The first hall is devoted to calligraphic rarities found in Cave No. 17 of the Mogao Grottoes. Paper documents have survived for a thousand years in the dry climate of the cave. In the second room, sacrificial objects unearthed in ancient tombs are shown alongside pots, a plough and armour. Ancient handicrafts displayed in the third hall include a Tang-Dynasty chess set, a present from the governor to the emperor.

Mogao Caves 莫高窟

In spite of the difficulties, tourists still head for this 2,000-year-old town to see China's most magnificent ancient murals and painted statues. Since you've come this far, they're worth another 25 kilometres (15 miles).

The Mogao Caves, hewn from a desert cliffside, tell the story of the great flowering of Buddhist art in China. Begun in the 4th century, they were created in fits and starts over the next thousand years. Statistics aren't everything, but consider that there are 45,000 square metres of mural paintings here—more than *ten acres* of walls and ceilings covered with brightly coloured pictures of men and gods and speculations about eternity. And in the same caves stand more than 2,000 painted sculptures, realistic or fantastic.

Of the several hundred grottoes still intact, only a few dozen are open to the public. And even these are kept locked so that visits may be supervised. The outer walls of the caves have been reinforced and walkways added.

Tours may cover various itineraries; here are some things to look out for:

Northern Wei Dynasty (A.D. 386–534). Statues with Persian or Indian faces; graceful, lifelike **animal paintings;** three-dimensional effects.

Sui Dynasty (A.D. 581–618). Illustrations of religious stories; notice the emotions revealed in the characters' faces, and that Chinese robes have replaced foreign dress.

Tang Dynasty (A.D. 618–907). Don't miss Cave No. 96, a nine-storey temple from the 7th century. The **seated Buddha** statue inside has toes as long as your arm. Cave No. 158 is filled with a statue of the **reclining Buddha,** the face unusually peaceful and godly when seen from the far left. You'll be struck by the imagination, life and colour of the **Tang wall paintings.**

Later Dynasties. **Murals** from the 10th century onwards give valuable details of everyday life in medieval China.

Crescent Moon Lake
月牙湖

Most of the desert is grey and menacing—a sea of gravel out of which stark rocky mountains occasionally appear. But everybody's dream desert may be seen a few kilometres south of Dunhuang. With oases in sight, awesome dunes rise in waves. As the sun and clouds move, the colours and textures of the sand hills change.

Hidden between the hills is a small, clear lake—Crescent Moon Lake *(Yue Ya Hu)*. It's not a mirage. Reeds grow at the edge of this cool blue spring and tiny fish swim in it. You can reach the lake from the edge of the desert on the back of a camel, or, if you like walking in sand, afoot. Twenty minutes each way should do it. For a rare desert experience, climb to the top of a dune and listen to the musical—or thunderous—sound as the sand slides down.

FOSHAN 佛山

The silk, porcelain and handicrafts centre of Foshan first came to national attention during the Tang Dynasty, when three Buddha statues were carved into a local hillside. (Foshan means "Buddha Hill".) In modern times the artisans of the town (population nearly 300,000) have retained their reputation, even while investment has been directed to new engineering, electronic and chemical industries.

Only 20 kilometres (12 miles) from Guangzhou (Canton), Foshan is the goal of many day trips from the metropolis of the Pearl River delta — with which it shares a winterless climate.

Whatever the weather, the local sightseeing highlight is the Song-Dynasty **Ancestral Temple** *(Zu Miao)*, rebuilt in 1372 and again in the 1970s. This Daoist temple, a work of extravagant beauty, unites many ancient art forms and materials: wood, brick, stone, ceramics and bronze. A surrounding park contains pavilions, towers, gates, gardens and a lotus pool. On exhibit out of doors is an array of the ceremonial weapons used by guards of honour in ancient times, standing in a sort of umbrella rack.

Tourists are usually taken to a **ceramics factory** in nearby Shiwan township, but not to see how bricks and building tiles are turned out. Porcelain figurines,

Farmers rely on pedal power, too.

birds and animals are the factory's proudest products, and visitors follow the manufacturing process from conception through to the painting, firing and glazing.

At the **Folk Art Institute** workers may be seen making such traditional handicrafts as Chinese lanterns, or carving sculptures,

painting scrolls and cutting intricate designs in paper (Foshan paper-cuts go back to the 10th century). A cross-section of all these products is on sale in the company store.

Silk is another local speciality. By request, visits may be made to a **silk mill** where the fabric is woven, dyed and printed. But the modern industrial installation is a far cry from the cottage industry of old.

GUANGZHOU 广州 (CANTON)

Foreigners have been turning up in Guangzhou for a couple of thousand years, for it was China's first major seaport. This has made for some dramatic historical incidents, such as the Opium Wars, which broke out when the authorities cracked down on the opium trade here.

In spite of the problems, this crowded city maintains its gate-

GUANGZHOU (CANTON)

way role. Ever since 1957 the Canton Trade Fair has attracted throngs of international businessmen. Originally held biannually, it has now become a permanent fixture at the Guangzhou Foreign Trade Centre. Even in the years of political upheaval, Guangzhou kept open the nation's ties with foreign countries and with overseas Chinese, millions of whom have their roots in Guangdong Province.

Guangzhou straddles the Pearl River, China's fifth longest river, which links the metropolis to the South China Sea. The waterway provides a good deal of charm and excitement; the daily drama of ferryboats, freighters, junks with dirty grey sails, low-lying sampans—even small tankers and big gunboats—unfolds right in the centre of town. The river also irrigates surrounding farmlands, which yield a cornucopia of rice, fruit and vegetables.

With a population above 5 million, Guangzhou is primarily an industrial city of more than 3,200 factories. Production lines turn out buses, ships, agricultural machinery, chemicals and sewing machines. Although the economy has changed radically in recent

Chinese from Hong Kong, across the way, keep Guangzhou's discos hopping.

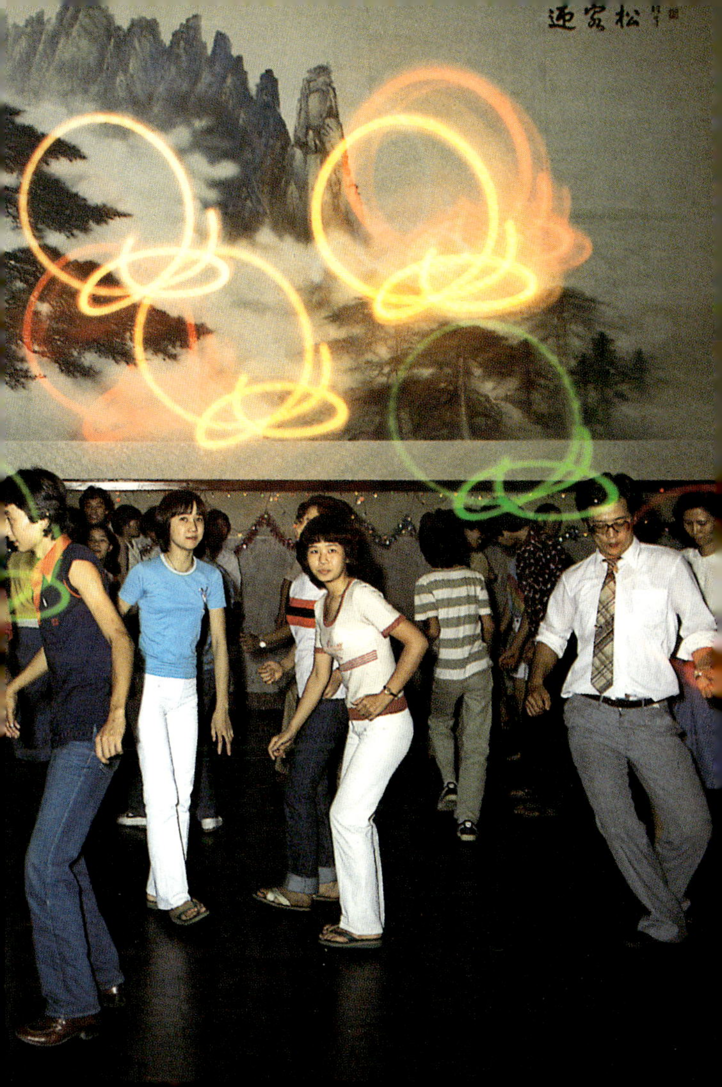
迎客松

years, many local traditions live on: the love of flowers, Cantonese Opera, the local dialect (incomprehensible to fellow Chinese). And then there is Cantonese food, much appreciated in its adaptations around the world but unexcelled when created in its home kitchen.

Canton in History

In the 3rd century B.C. the founder of the Qin Dynasty annexed the remote Guangzhou area, furnishing China with its first major seaport. By the end of the Han Dynasty, foreign trade linked the port with other areas of Asia, as well as with the Roman Empire. The name Guangzhou was bestowed during the Kingdom of Wu (3rd century A.D.), but foreigners came to call it Canton.

As commerce expanded, so did the foreign population of the port. By the 9th century a large colony of Arabs, Jews, Persians and other merchants had settled here. They traded in tea, silk and porcelain—Chinese products in constant demand abroad.

It was another seven centuries before Europeans established themselves in Canton. The Portuguese were first, followed by Spaniards, Dutch and English. The Chinese authorities endeavoured to keep the foreigners at arm's length, limiting their activities to certain districts and seasons.

The expansion of trade eventually brought conflict, for China would accept nothing less than silver bullion in payment for its exports. But the wily British thought of an alternative commodity—opium (see page 35). The Opium Wars ended in 1842 with the Treaty of Nanking (later denounced as "unequal"). Under the terms of the treaty, China was compelled to open Canton and four other ports to foreign penetration.

The ever shakier Manchu Dynasty fell in 1911, to be replaced by the Chinese Republic, founded by a native of Guangdong Province, Dr. Sun Yat-sen. In 1927, the Communist-led forces who established the Guangzhou Commune were wiped out by the troops of Chiang Kai-shek.

During World War II the Japanese occupied Guangzhou. In the subsequent civil war, Guangzhou briefly served as the Nationalist capital before the Communists captured the city and gained power nationwide in 1949.

Sightseeing

Guangzhou doesn't claim to compete with Beijing or Xi'an when it comes to sightseeing sensations. But its monuments and parks are well worth visiting, not least for the chance to mingle with the Cantonese themselves.

Yue Xiu Park, near the Trade Fair in the northern part of the city, covers a hilly 93 hectares (230 acres). Along with pretty gardens, lakes, pavilions and sports facilities, Guangzhou's largest park contains one of the city's oldest buildings, the red **Tower Overlooking the Sea** *(Zhen Hai Lou)*. Actually, "tower" is a misleading description for this verandahed building of five storeys. Built in 1380, it now houses the municipal museum, devoted to Guangzhou's history and art. Prehistoric items are displayed on the ground floor, with more recent material on the floors above.

An equally famous but modern landmark in the park is a granite sculptural representation of five handsome goats. Legend says the city of Guangzhou was founded thus: five gods descended from heaven riding goats which held sprigs of rice in their mouths. The celestial visitors distributed the rice, blessing the local people with eternal freedom from famine. The gods thereupon disappeared, according to the story, but the five rice-bearing goats turned to stone. And here they are—or at least their replicas.

Dr. Sun Yat-sen (1866–1925), who began his political career in the city, is honoured in Yue Xiu Park by an **obelisk** 30 metres (about 100 feet) tall. South of the park is an even more impressive monument to the statesman, the **Sun Yat-sen Memorial Hall,** built in 1931. This vast, modern version of a traditional Chinese building, with its sweeping blue-tile roofs, contains an auditorium big enough to seat close to 5,000 people.

Guangzhou's prime Buddhist monument, the **Temple of the Six Banyan Trees** *(Liu Rong Si)*, was founded more than 1,400 years ago. The trees that inspired the 11th-century poet and calligrapher, Su Dongpo, to name the temple have died, but the often-restored complex remains a focus of local Buddhist activities. Overlooking it all is the **Flower Pagoda** *(Hua Ta)*, a slender relic of the Song Dynasty. From the outside, the pagoda appears to be nine storeys high, but there are really 17 floors inside.

In the early Middle Ages, Canton had a significant Muslim population owing to trade with the Middle East. This is how it came to pass that the city has what's said to be the oldest mosque in China, the **Huai Sheng Mosque,** traditionally dated A.D. 627. It has been rebuilt in modern time and after a hiatus during the upheavals of the Cultural Revolution, again serves the small local Muslim community.

Another religious edifice that suffered during the 1960s and '70s is the Roman Catholic **Cathedral.** Red Guards converted the century-old, Gothic-style church into a warehouse, but the cathedral was reconsecrated in 1979.

The feeling of 19th-century Canton is best evoked by **Shamian Island,** in the Pearl River, linked to central Guangzhou by two bridges. This small residential enclave, shaded by banyan trees, was the closed community of the foreign colony in the era of the Western "concessions". The stately, European-style buildings have been taken over as government offices, headquarters of foreign legations or as public housing. The island, haunted by nostalgia, has a fresh claim to tourist attention—a luxury hotel, big and modern.

A popular, optional excursion is an hour's detour to the Guangzhou **Zoo,** founded in 1958. More than 200 animal species are represented: Manchurian tigers, white-lipped deer and the famous giant panda. The zoo also boasts an imaginative monkey mountain behind a moat, where dozens of uninhibited chimps cavort for appreciative crowds.

The **Pearl River** itself makes a good excursion. The local branch of China International Travel Service runs special cruises for foreign tourists aboard a large, comfortable sightseeing boat. The sights—shipyard, White Swan Hotel, Nanfang Department Store and the bridges—are identified over the loudspeakers in English and other languages. But most memorable of all are the swarms of sampans and junks plying this river, just as they have done over the centuries.

On any tour of the Pearl River delta you can see the rich fields of rice, vegetables and fruit trees; the river itself and the nearby South China Sea complement the bounty with a wide variety of seafood. The availability and proximity of all the raw materials is one good reason that Cantonese food tastes so special in its native city—light years away from the simulations so prevalent abroad.

Revolutionary Monuments

Guided tours of Guangzhou usually include one or more of the sites linked with the history of the Chinese revolution:

The **National Peasant Movement Institute,** housed in a former Confucian temple, served as a training school for the Chinese Communist Party in the 1920s. Mao Zedong himself directed the institute in 1926 and gave lectures on geography, rural education, and "The Problem of the Chinese Peasantry". Zhou Enlai taught here, too.

Martyrs' Memorial Park—more formally the Memorial Park to the Martyrs of the Guangzhou Uprising—was dedicated on the 30th anniversary of the doomed insurrection of December 11, 1927. The armed uprising against the Kuomintang, led by the Communist Party, was crushed within three days at a cost of more than 5,000 lives. With spacious lawns and flower gardens, palm trees and pavilions, the park proves an unexpectedly relaxed place to watch the local people strolling, courting, airing their babies, or playing Chinese checkers.

Another memorial park surrounds the **Mausoleum of the 72 Martyrs,** dedicated to victims of one of the insurrections that failed in 1911, only months before Dr. Sun Yat-sen's successful revolution. The design of the monumental ensemble has something for everyone: Chinese lions, an Egyptian obelisk, and even a model of the Statue of Liberty.

Olives are a thriving industry in the warm south.

GUILIN 桂林
(Kweilin)

China's most "Chinese" scenery, the subject of thousands of paintings, is to be found in Guilin. The "finest mountains and rivers under heaven" are so inspiring that poets, artists and tourists can't stay away—even when heaven lets rip with cascades of rain that hide the hills.

The climate here is subtropical, with an annual rainfall of 1,900 mm. (75 inches). If you can avoid the rainiest season, April through July, the odds for good weather greatly improve. An additional incentive for visiting in autumn is the sight and fragrance of osmanthus (cassia) blossoms all over town. (The name Guilin means "Cassia Woods".)

Tourists are so commonplace in the otherwise relaxed shopping district of Guilin that the pedestrian crossings are signposted in English as well as Chinese. Another cosmopolitan influence comes from the area's many tribesmen; Guilin is part of the Guangxi-Zhuang Autonomous Region, which borders Vietnam. The proliferation of so-called Muslim restaurants is explained by the presence of thousands of members of the traditionally Muslim Zhuang nationality, China's largest minority group.

The geological history of Guilin—the key to the wonder of its moody mountains and caves—goes back several hundred million years. The area was under the sea, we are told, when an upheaval raised it to the status of terra firma. But later it was flooded, then lifted again in further cataclysmic events. The alternation of sea water and air through the millennia created limestone formations called karst, vulnerable to erosion into pinnacles and mounds and peaks that captivate the imagination.

The history of Guilin began more than 2,000 years ago when the Ling canal was built, effectively linking the great Yangtze and Pearl rivers. Guilin's connection with one of mankind's most ambitious engineering projects was important, but otherwise, little was heard about the town. It served as provincial capital for several hundred years. Thanks to the profusion of caves to hide in, Guilin was a centre for resistance during the war with Japan. Today, rebuilt from the rubble of war, the city looks as if it's thriving, thanks to manufacturing industries, agriculture and—obviously—tourism.

Every rock round Guilin has its legend: at Elephant Trunk Hill a celestial elephant, turned to stone, drinks forever from the river.

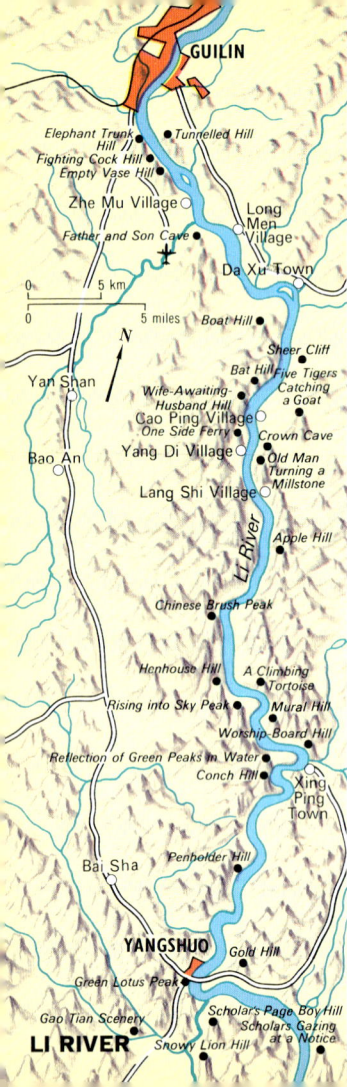

Map labels

GUILIN

Elephant Trunk Hill
Fighting Cock Hill
Empty Vase Hill
Zhe Mu Village
Father and Son Cave

Tunnelled Hill

Long Men Village

Da Xu Town

0 ___ 5 km
0 ___ 5 miles

N

Boat Hill

Yan Shan

Sheer Cliff
Bat Hill Five Tigers
Wife-Awaiting Catching
Husband Hill a Goat
Gao Ping Village
One Side Ferry
Yang Di Village Crown Cave
Old Man
Turning a
Bao An Millstone
Lang Shi Village

Apple Hill

Li River

Chinese Brush Peak

Henhouse Hill A Climbing
Tortoise
Rising into Sky Peak Mural Hill
Worship-Board Hill
Reflection of Green Peaks in Water
Conch Hill
Xing
Ping
Town

Bai Sha Penholder Hill

YANGSHUO
Gold Hill
Green Lotus Peak
Scholars Page Boy Hill
Gao Tian Scenery Scholars Gazing
at a Notice
LI RIVER Snowy Lion Hill

On the River

The transcendent tourist experience of Guilin — and maybe of all China — is a **boat trip** on the Li River. The karst scenery, of course, couldn't be more romantic. But life along the river also fascinates: washerwomen squatting on the shore, water-buffalo ambling down for a dip, the improvised ferryboats, and the captive cormorants, their necks ringed, perched on rafts, waiting for orders to go fishing.

Tourist boats usually leave early in the morning from the quay near the Liberation Bridge in central Guilin. (In the dry season, when the river is at its lowest, the first part of the journey must be undertaken by coach.) Big, modern boats, with room for more than 100 passengers each, are pulled by tugs — eliminating the noise and vibration of ship engines. But the smaller boats are self-propelled.

Even before leaving town the spectacle begins. On the right bank is **Elephant Trunk Hill,** the first of many peaks that romantics have endowed with animal or supernatural identities. It takes no great imagination to see the resemblance of this outcrop to an elephant drinking in the river; the space between the trunk and the body has been hollowed through. River traffic, meanwhile, keeps amateur photographers snapping in all directions: scows and hand-poled bamboo rafts, sampans and towboats.

A sampling of images as the boat continues southward: Tunnelled Hill, Pagoda Hill (also known as Battleship Hill), Washing Vase Hill, and Fighting Cocks Hills (facing each other from opposite banks of the river). A large village on the left bank, Dragon Gate Village, is noted for water chestnuts and its thousand-year-old banyan tree.

Beyond is a much larger village, Da Xu, with a high bridge from the Ming period, called **Longevity Bridge.** The town has been a regional commercial centre for hundreds of years.

Opposite Da Xu, and in other areas along the river, the rich, flat land produces the ingredients for a formidable fruit salad—oranges and grapefruit, chestnuts and persimmons, plus exotic tropical delicacies all but unknown outside Asia. Adding to the entrancing beauty of the scene, great stands of a feathery variety of bamboo grow along the riverbanks.

Beyond the village of Yang Di unfolds the kind of scenery described by a Chinese poet more than a thousand years ago: "The river is a green silk belt, the mountains emerald hairpins". Peaks and pinnacles crowd the river, white goats pose on steep mountainsides, and an eagle soars above the cliffs. The river itself flows green and transparent, inviting even on a rainy day. Credit for this limpid rarity goes not only to the strict antipollution programme to protect the River Li, but also to nature itself, which endows the water with a high content of carbonic acid.

Mural Hill is so called because the sheer cliff face comprises so many patches of colour that it might be a fresco. In the lights and shadows of the cliff, the shapes of nine different horses can be discerned, hence the cliff's alternate name, Nine Horse Hill.

The commune of Xinping, on the left, is surrounded by magic scenery—landmarks with names like Snail Hill, Five Fingers Hill and Carp Hill.

The boat trips end at the county town of **Yangshuo,** famous for its own hill called **Green Lotus Peak,** a favourite of poets and painters. The distance traversed totals 83 kilometres (52 miles). The trip back to Guilin by car or bus gives a different perspective on the verdant scenery.

Touring the Town

The best way to appreciate Guilin's unique setting is to climb to the summit of the hill called **Die Cai Shan,** on the north side of town. The name means Piled Silk Hill or folded Brocade Hill—a metaphor suggested by the layers of rock. Yet another name is Cassia Tree Hill.

Hiking to the lookout point at the top of the hill is rather strenuous, but catching your breath is only one of the good reasons for stopping along the way. For instance, there is **Breezy Cave,** cutting through the hill from south to north. It is permanently cooled by a refreshing breeze, to the relief of grateful crowds on hot summer days. The many inscriptions carved into the cave walls over the centuries are much admired by connoisseurs of calligraphy.

At the summit—altitude 223 metres (732 feet) above sea level—the charmingly named **Catch-Cloud Pavilion** *(Na Yun Ting)* provides a 360-degree panorama. The view is to be savoured: the winding river, the cityscape, fertile flat farmland, and the surreal hills forever popping up both in town and country.

Closer to the centre of the city is another hill with a view and other distractions—**Fubo Hill,** or Whirlpool Hill. According to legend, a General Fubo, who passed this way 2,000 years ago, tested his sword here. Thus **Sword-Testing Stone** is a stalactite formation that comes down to within inches of the ground, as if the general's sword had sliced through the bottom of the pillar. Further on, the

Peanut pickers work against time—and the mysterious backdrop of the Guilin hills.

Thousand Buddha Cliff is carved with several hundred figures, dating from the Tang and Song dynasties.

The **District of the Two Lakes** in the southern part of town has been made into a delightful public park with gardens, walkways and pagodas. Originally, Banyan Tree Lake *(Rong Hu)* and Fir Tree Lake *(Sha Hu)* were a single expanse, forming part of the moat which protected the city wall. The Song-Dynasty Green Belt Bridge across the middle created the two lakes.

Around Guilin, you'll find caves of every size and mood—gloomy, inspiring, immense or cosy. Most tourist itineraries take in one of the two best known caves—Reed Flute or Seven Star, on opposite sides of town.

Reed Flute Cave *(Lu Di Yan)* burrows deep into a hill, while on the surface grow reeds suitable for making flutes, hence the name. The visions within are weird indeed. They benefit from good lighting effects. As in most other caverns, certain formations have been given poetic names. Apart from Virgin Forest and Giant Lion, there is one huge rock that suggests the form of an Old Scholar, seated in contemplation of a simulated waterfall across the way. According to legend, a scholar once tried to write a poem worthy of the cave's beauty, but before he could find adequate words he had turned to stone. The cave's largest chamber, the **Crystal Palace** can accommodate a thousand people. Bats inhabit the darker recesses, but the eerie waters that flow through the cave are devoid of fish.

Seven Star Cave *(Qi Xing Yan)*, is a mere million years old. It has been a tourist attraction for more than a thousand years. Some of the scenic formations of stalactites and stalagmites have names like Old Banyan Tree Welcoming Guests and Dragon Splashing Water, providing an idea of the poetic licence enjoyed by Chinese cave explorers. The round trip inside this cave is considerably longer than the itinerary in the Reed Flute Cave. Both underworlds have constant, comfortable temperatures year-round but they are dripping with a humidity that makes the going slippery.

All around town you'll see Chinese tourists proudly carrying unusual walking sticks, fashioned from a bamboo shaft with a square cross-section. The unusual species grows in an inaccessible mountain area.

There may be some foods you wouldn't touch with a barge pole, let alone bamboo chopsticks. Guilin's local delicacies include masked civet, pangolin (scaly anteater), and "ground goat"—a euphemism for dog meat, a favourite of Chinese gourmets for thousands of years.

HANGZHOU 杭州
(Hangchow)

Several dozen lakes in China are named West Lake, but only one is so celebrated it needs no further identification: West Lake *(Xi Hu)* in Hangzhou.

The Song-Dynasty poet Su Dongpo likened the lake to one of ancient China's greatest beauties, Xi Zi—who was also calm, soft, delicate and enchanting, even unadorned in the mist and rain. (The girls of Hangzhou are still famous for their light, clear complexion, which is attributed to the mild, humid climate.)

But Hangzhou has more than scenery. A city of over a million people, rich in historic and cultural monuments, it also offers visitors some educational outings: here you can see how two of China's most delightful inven-

tions—silk and tea—are produced.

Historically, Hangzhou enjoyed 237 years of imperial glory, from the 9th century onwards. In all, 14 kings and emperors held court here. When Marco Polo visited in the 13th century he pronounced the city superior to "all others in the world, in grandeur and beauty, as well as... its abundant delights, which might lead an inhabitant to imagine himself in paradise".

Hangzhou is the southern terminus of the world's first canal (and the longest one in use), the Grand Canal. The capital of Zhejiang Province, Hangzhou is 189 kilometres (117 miles) from Shanghai—about three hours on the train, making it a possible, though rather exhausting, day trip.

West Lake 西湖

For a full panorama of West Lake and the city as well, travel up to the viewing platforms at a pavilion atop **Wu Hill** *(Wu Shan)*, south of the lake. The hilltop setting is richly forested with gingko, maple and camphor trees.

But the beauty of the lake can best be appreciated at close range—from the deck of a sightseeing boat or from the paths of the park along its shore. The park is abundantly supplied with flowers and trees and, unusually for China, secluded places where lovers can find privacy (but only until the 11 p.m. closing time, when everyone must leave).

The great themes of Buddhism are carved deep into the rock at Ling Yin Temple near Hangzhou.

The highlight of boat trips is the largest of three man-made islands in the Outer Lake, a "small fairy island" known as **Three Pools Mirroring the Moon** *(San Yan Yin Yue)*. Ingeniously, the island—created in the Ming Dynasty—is provided with an island of its own, in the centre of its own lake. A zigzag bridge will get you there. Three small stone pagodas, rebuilt in the 17th century, rise from the main lake just south of the isle. On the night of the Moon Festival, candles are placed inside the pagodas. The flickering light emanating from the small round windows gives the lake 15 reflections imitating the real moon.

Solitary Hill *(Gu Shan)*, in the northern part of the lake, is reached from the city by a causeway named after a Tang-Dynasty poet, Bai Juyi. In the 9th century he was demoted from a high imperial post to the job of governor of Hangzhou because he wrote poems satirizing the court. This made him popular with the ordinary people. The hillsides are brightened by trees and flowers and pavilions.

From Monastery to Plantation

One of the best known Buddhist monasteries in the country, Hangzhou's **Ling Yin Temple** (meaning "Spirits' Retreat"), attracts crowds of Chinese tourists and believers. The monks—for this is a working monastery—are kept busy supplying joss sticks to devout or merely fun-loving visitors. The main hall contains a **statue** of the Buddha, seated on a lotus leaf. Carved of camphor-wood, it is 19½ metres (64 feet) high and called the largest such sculpture in China.

Trips to agricultural communes and industrial plants may not be everybody's choice, but the following excursions offer real insights into Chinese life.

A brigade of the **West Lake Commune** cultivates tea. Handily, the bushes grow only a few steps from the building where tourists are given a mug of green tea and a briefing. The excursion includes a walk through the drying rooms. The choice leaves are hand-dried in electric woks—a hot job and potentially damaging to the hands. Other grades are processed by machine.

The Hangzhou Silk Printing and Dyeing Complex claims to be the biggest **silk factory** in China, and maybe in all of Asia. It employs 5,600 people, mostly women. Tours follow production from the sorting of cocoons, which arrive by barge in 20-kilogramme (44-pound) sacks, to the silk-screen printing process. At the end of the line is a shop where foreign visitors, exploiting their newly gained expertise, browse through the bolts of silk.

HARBIN 哈尔滨

Only an Eskimo, you'd think, could survive winter in Harbin, the capital of China's north-easternmost province, Heilongjiang. The average temperature stays below freezing five months of the year, and in January the mercury has been known to descend to −38°C. (−36°F).

In a country of ancient cities, Harbin is an anomaly. Until the turn of the 20th century it never amounted to more than a fishing village. Then the Manchu Dynasty agreed to let Tsarist Russia build a branch of the Trans-Siberian Railway through Harbin. Russians and other foreigners peopled the fast-growing transportation hub, which soon boasted hotels and banks, bars and gambling houses.

With the Bolshevik revolution of 1917, perhaps half a million Russian emigrés fled through Siberia to Harbin, consolidating the Russian appearance of the city with more pastel-coloured stucco houses and churches with onion domes. From 1932 to 1945 Harbin was under Japanese occupation, followed by one year under the Soviet army. In 1946 the Chinese

Coloured lights give a magic glow to Harbin's ice sculptures.

Communists took control of the city. Under the People's Republic, Harbin has become an important industrial centre as well as the heart of a rich grain-producing area.

The mighty **Songhua River,** running through Harbin from east to west, inevitably engages tourist attention. In summer there are sightseeing launches and, for the brave, swimming. On the south bank, **Stalin Park** has many recreational facilities. So does **Sun Island** (*Tai Yang Dao*) in the middle of the river, an amalgam of health resorts, beach installations and gardens.

In town, **Children's Park** is the site of a miniature railway operated by children — the only one of its kind in China. The small trains carry passengers of all ages between "Harbin Station" and "Beijing Station" — a distance of 2 kilometres (just over a mile). In real life the distance is 1,388 kilometres (862 miles).

At the Lunar New Year, or Spring Festival (late January or early February), Harbin puts on a spectacular show rivalling the Snow Festival of its sister city in Japan, Sapporo. While the rest of China is celebrating with paper lanterns, Harbin is showing off with lanterns carved out of ice. Delicate sculptures and whole buildings made of ice are brilliantly illuminated. It's so festive you might almost forget the cold.

HOHHOT 呼和浩特
(*Huhehot*)

The capital of the Inner Mongolia Autonomous Region, Hohhot is a sprawling, booming city with a metropolitan population of more than one million. The centre of town looks to the future with new official buildings, housing blocks and wide avenues, but the traffic evokes nostalgia: a pageant of donkey carts, ox carts, pony carts and farm tractors, plus the usual proliferation of bicycles.

It may come as a surprise that Mongolians are a small minority here. Most of the residents of Hohhot are Han (ethnic Chinese); Inner Mongolia's close connection with China dates back several centuries. For tourists in search of the exotic, though, Hohhot and vicinity offer many opportunities to make contact with Mongolian traditions. You can drink butter tea with millet and sleep in a yurt — a felt-covered circular tent.

An unexpected feature of Hohhot is its modern racecourse. Under the sky-blue domes of the reviewing stand, groups of tourists are treated to a Mongolian "rodeo" of racing and trick riding and perhaps a march-past of two-humped camels.

For a less contrived variety of local colour, call in at the **free market,** where pedlars shout their wares with equal enthusiasm, whether they're selling shirts or vegetables or sunglasses. Cobblers work hand-cranked sewing machines in the open air. A bard, banging a cymbal, chants a story, while his partner—a trained monkey—dons the masks and hats of Chinese opera characters. The crowd is entranced.

Five pagodas stand on the roof of the aptly named **Five Pagodas Temple** *(Wu Ta Si)*, a striking 18th-century structure. Buddhist scriptures are inscribed on the outer wall in Sanskrit, Tibetan and Mongolian, along with carvings of 1,600 figures.

It's estimated that 20,000 Muslims live in Hohhot. The **Great Mosque,** built in the Ming Dynasty, has a minaret that culminates in a Chinese-style temple roof (topped by a crescent). The front of the prayer hall is adorned with Arabic inscriptions and ceramic abstractions.

Hohhot's oldest historical site, 17 kilometres (11 miles) southwest of town, is the **Tomb of Princess Zhao Jun.** In 33 B.C., at the age of 18, this famous Chinese beauty married a tribal chief, bringing about what is now hailed as peace among the nationalities. You can stroll to the top of the 33-metre (98-foot) hill built above her grave and look out at the endless, flat farmland.

South-east of Hohhot is the 12th-century **White Pagoda,** known in Chinese as Wan Bu Hua Yan Jing Ta—the Pagoda of the Ten Thousand Scriptures. The seven-storey octagonal structure stands all alone in farmland. Once part of a Buddhist temple complex, it is now being fully restored following the depredations of wind, snow and the Cultural Revolution.

The Grasslands

The most memorable part of a visit to Hohhot is likely to be an excursion to the grasslands, across the desolate Daqing Mountains. A good paved road eases the strain of the zigzag climb that reaches about 2,000 metres (more than 6,500 feet) above sea level. (Photography is forbidden in these mountains, which are riddled with military installations facing the sensitive border with the Mongolian People's Republic.)

The **Red Banner Commune,** in the wide open spaces 86 kilometres (53 miles) north-west of Hohhot, is dedicated to animal husbandry, with a profitable sideline in tourism. Some 200 tourists can be accommodated in special luxury felt tents or yurts. Each structure has sleeping platforms covered with oriental rugs; there's a thermos for tea and a coal stove, kept going all night by a local retainer who pops in unannounced.

Visitors are treated to an informal rodeo in which Mongolian horsemen race their energetic ponies. Disarmingly, the cowboys are dressed like any ordinary Chinese farmer. Tourists are then offered the chance to ride camels (stepladders are provided for mounting the mild-mannered animals) and ponies.

The commune occupies land that is mostly desert in winter, but beautiful green pastureland in summer; it supports more than 2,000 people and 45,000 animals. Tourists are invited to visit a "typical" farmhouse, to sit shoeless and cross-legged on the raised platform which serves as the family bed, to taste Mongolian snacks and drink bowls of milk tea and listen to sad songs. Like all the other houses on the plain, it faces south, turning its windowless back to the cruel north winds.

Travellers with more time to spare can venture a hundred kilometres further into the wilderness, where another commune claims to offer greener scenery and the experience of sleeping in a *real* yurt, not one specially furnished for foreigners.

Sheep-rearing is a family affair for Kazakh nomads, who roam the desert lands of Inner Mongolia.

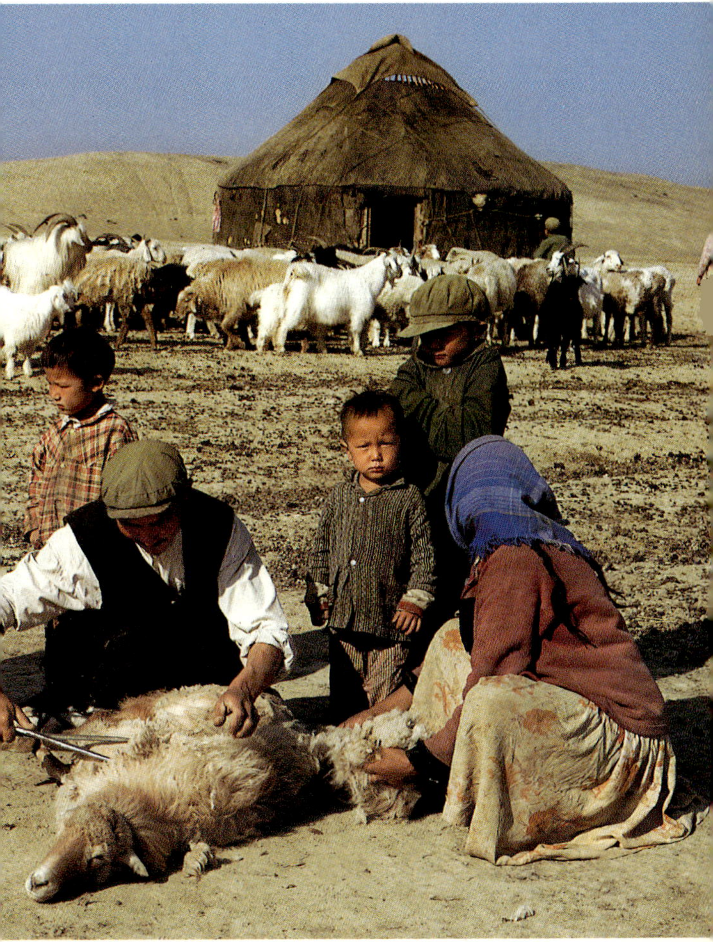

HUANG SHAN 黄山
(Hwang Shan)

"Yellow Mountain" may be the literal translation of Huang Shan (which is not one mountain but a range of dozens of peaks), but in spite of the name, yellow is not the colour that first comes to mind when describing this romantic scenery — the stuff of Chinese poetry and painting for centuries. In reality, green is the colour of the stunted pines clinging to purple cliff faces. Pink are the wild flowers, blue the sky, and white the sea of clouds that rolls in beneath the rocky pinnacles.

Huang Shan is the only part of eastern China's Anhui Province that appears on major tourist itineraries. Trains and planes link Shanghai with a terminus at the foot of the mountains, from where coaches continue the journey. The scenic resort now has hotel facilities, from extremely basic to comfortable, for thousands of guests. Chinese tourists — and poets — spend a week or more exploring the mountains, but foreign tourists try to squeeze it all into three days.

The weather, of course, makes a crucial contribution — or obstacle — to the pleasure of mountain rambles and sightseeing. On average, mid-July to the end of September is considered the most dependable time of year because of the mild temperatures and relatively restrained rainfall. Drizzle rather than heavy rain generally falls from late May to late June, when the spring flowers burst forth, but temperatures are brisk.

Huang Shan has many peaks which are well known by name in China. But the three principal summits are **Lotus Flower Peak** *(Lian Hua Feng)*, **Bright Summit** *(Guang Ming Ding)*, and the **Heavenly Capital Peak** *(Tian Du Feng)*. All are above 1,800 metres (6,000 feet).

When hiking becomes too strenuous, Huang Shan visitors can recuperate in a **hot spring resort** between Purple Cloud Peak *(Zi Yun Feng)* and Peach Blossom Peak *(Tao Hua Feng)*. Piping hot water with a curative mineral content bubbles from the spring year-round. You can drink it, bathe in it, or both.

The Huang Shan phenomenon that has most inspired painters and photographers is the sight of cottony clouds nuzzling the mountainsides. The peaks and pinnacles, jutting above the clouds in the early morning sky, look like islets in a celestial sea. They've even gone to the trouble of building a lookout for the best possible view. In the unavoidable Chinese combination of prose and poetry, it's called the **Cloud-Dispersing Pavilion.**

Huang Shan peaks float like islands in a sea of cloud.

JINAN 济南
(Tsinan)

Sweet water gushes from more than 100 springs within the city limits of Jinan, the capital of Shandong (Shantung) Province. The water enhances agriculture and industry and even turns the City of Springs, as it is sometimes called, into something of a tourist attraction. And thanks to nature's generosity, Jinan is the only city in China where you can safely drink the tap water. Even so, most tourists only pass through Jinan on their way to the traditional sights of Shandong, such as the holy mountain, Taishan (see page 196), and the birthplace of Confucius, Qufu (see page 195).

The Jinan area seems to have been inhabited since the New Stone Age. More than 2,500 years ago a town wall was built. Jinan has been a prosperous provincial capital since the Middle Ages. At the turn of the 20th century the Manchu Dynasty granted foreign concessions in Jinan, prompting an influx of Europeans. The city was a focus of bitter fighting during the Chinese Civil War. Today more than a million people live in the city.

Sightseeing starts among the weeping willows along the shores of the **Lake of Great Light** (*Da Ming Hu*), in the northern part of the old city. In recent years the lake has been dredged and stone embankments built. All around the circumference are parks, playgrounds and pavilions.

As a name, **Thousand Buddha Mountain** (*Qian Fo Shan*), just south-east of the city, exaggerates more than a little: instead of a thousand Buddha images, you'll find a few dozen. As for the "mountain" qualification, it's only 280 metres (about 900 feet) above sea level. But a hike up the hill and down again permits a close look at a couple of ancient temples, grottoes with Buddhist statues, and refreshing forests.

Of all the springs in Jinan, the one with the most historical associations is the **Jet Spring** (*Bao Tu Quan*). In the 17th century the Qing-Dynasty Emperor Kangxi took a swig and pronounced it the "First Spring Under Heaven". It is now surrounded by a carefully landscaped park.

The fastest flowing spring of Jinan, **Black Tiger Spring** (*Hei Hu Quan*), is a short walk away. The sweet water rushes from the mouths of three tigers carved in a black stone cliffside; the cascade flows so noisily that it sounds to some like the roar of tigers.

As the provincial capital, Jinan is the site of the **Shandong Provincial Museum**, where more than 400,000 items illustrate local history and nature. The highlight of the collection is an exhibition of Longshan Black Pottery found near Jinan — an elegant, delicate ware fired 4,000 years ago.

120

KAIFENG 开封

The ancient walled city of Kaifeng, in eastern Henan (Honan) Province, lies near enough to the unpredictable Yellow River to have known more than its share of catastrophes. And when it wasn't being flooded it was being pillaged. The most terrible of the invasions, in the 12th century, ended the dreams of the Northern Song Dynasty and left Kaifeng in ruins. All things considered, it's almost miraculous that several historic buildings have survived to this day. So, remarkably, has much of the city's old imperial dignity.

Kaifeng rose to fame more than 2,000 years ago during the Warring States period, when it was capital of the Kingdom of Wei (220–265). The city's most prosperous and glorious era, though, was from A.D. 960 to 1127, when it served as the Eastern Capital of the Northern Song Dynasty.

The **Iron Pagoda** *(Tie Ta)*, Kaifeng's best known symbol, only *looks* as if it's made of iron. The exterior walls are faced with glazed bricks and tiles of an iron-like hue. Built in 1049 and restored in modern times, it is a lucky 13 storeys tall. It was originally part of a 6th-century monastery complex, but the other buildings were washed away in one of the great floods of the 19th century.

Another relic of the Song Dynasty, the square and imposing **Po Ta** (Pagoda of the Po Family) reveals none of the high-flying grace of the Iron Pagoda. This may be excused by the fact that the top three storeys of the building collapsed several hundred years ago.

Near the old city wall in the north-west section of the city, the **Dragon Pavilion** *(Long Ting)* stands high above potential floodwaters. With its double-decker upswept golden roofs, the 17th-century pavilion was the scene of many an imperial ceremony.

The **Xiang Guo Monastery,** founded in the 6th century, has had a lively history: burned down, rebuilt, flooded out, and finally restored by the present administration as a cultural and recreational centre. Don't miss the carved and gilded **statue** of the "Thousand-Armed and Thousand-Eyed Buddha", which, unusually, has more than the advertised number of arms and eyes.

One curious historical footnote: in the Middle Ages a community of Jews migrated to Kaifeng. At one time there was a synagogue in the city, to which hundreds of citizens belonged. Though their descendants, now completed assimilated, may still live in Kaifeng, the synagogue and associated monuments no longer exist.

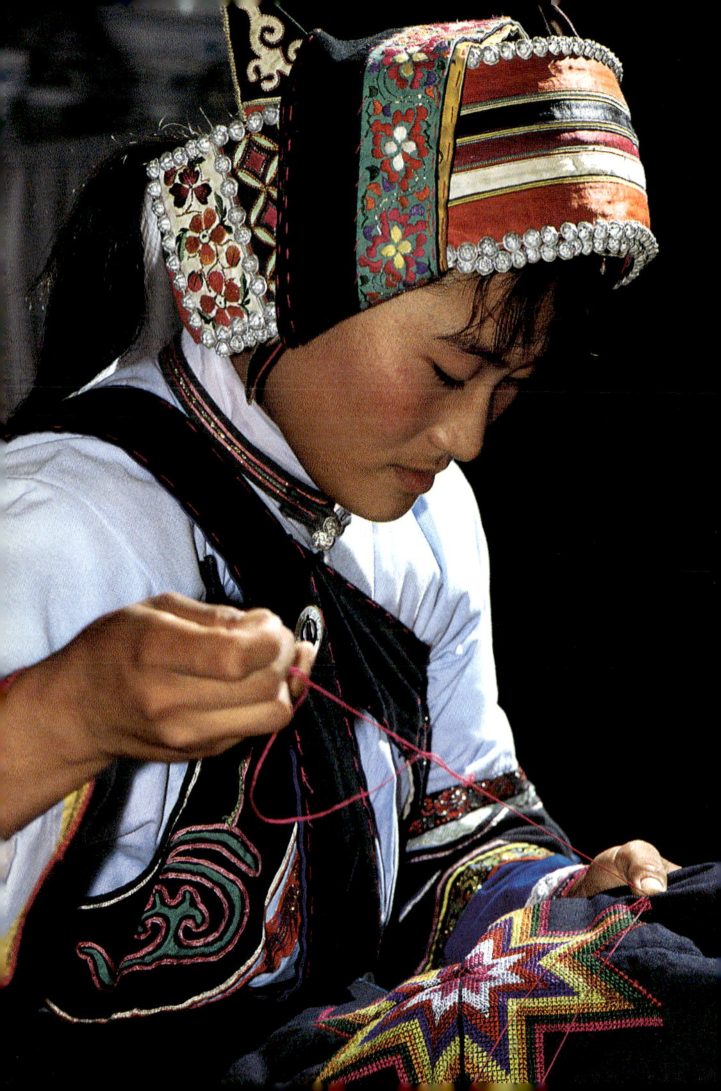

KUNMING 昆明

Flights to Kunming, the capital of Yunnan Province, land on an unexpectedly long runway with a dramatic history, commemorated neither by plaques nor monuments: this was once the end of the line for the Flying Tigers, the American pilots who supplied China "over the hump" in World War II. And Kunming was also the Chinese terminus for supplies travelling the tortuous Burma Road; milestone "0" — otherwise unmarked — may be seen on the right side of the road 21 kilometres (13 miles) from the centre of Kunming, on the edge of the Western Hills.

Kunming's most flaunted attraction is its benign climate. At an altitude of 1,894 metres (more than 6,200 feet) temperatures are pleasantly mild, producing what is described as year-round springtime. During one season or another the camelia, azalea, magnolia and begonia are in flower, and the rice farmers harvest three crops a year. The orchards grow anything from apples to oranges.

The metropolitan population stands at 2 million, of which half live in the city proper. Although Kunming claims a history of 2,000 years or more, urban development didn't really begin until the 19th century. Today broad new avenues shaded by pine and eucalyptus trees enclose warrens of traditional alleys. The morning rush hour is a chaos of bicycles, pony carts, hand-pulled carts, tractors and jeeps. To make it all the more exotic, a high proportion of the citizens belong to minority nationalities and often appear in ethnic costumes.

Kunming's prime scenic and recreational area surrounds **Lake Dian.** Boat trips for tourists, lasting two to three hours, explore the crystal waters. You'll also have the opportunity to go for a swim. The rich green slopes of the **Western Hills** rise along the far shore. Here you'll find the biggest temple of Kunming, **Hua Ting Temple,** founded in the Tang Dynasty. Just beyond the entrance is an outsize lotus pool, and the whole area is overrun with trees and flowers. The main hall has 500 polychrome ceramic figures along the side walls, representing Buddha's disciples. Some are posed eccentrically; others have been given such ugly faces you can hardly bear to look at them.

A strenuous climb up the hillside — 334 steps from the car-park — leads to **Dragon Gate** *(Long Men).* During the Ming Dynasty the emperor was carried all the way up from the lakeside by four bearers. There are several

Like China's other ethnic minorities, the Yi people take pride in their traditional costumes.

123

excellent places you can stop to catch your breath on the way up, including a teahouse, the former concubines' residence and the emperor's living quarters. The gate itself is only wide enough for one person to pass at a time. Caves painstakingly cut into the sheer mountainside contain colourfully painted carvings, all the work of a single-minded Daoist monk of the 18th century and his followers.

The Stone Forest 石林 (Shi Lin)

From Kunming it's a long drive of 120 kilometres (75 miles) southeast to the Stone Forest, an otherworldly fantasy hundreds of millions of years old, and still subject to change with every earthquake. Geologists say this natural wonder originated 200 million years ago, with the interaction of limestone, sea water, rainwater and seismic upheavals. The bizarre pinnacles that resulted are of the distinctive type of limestone called karst. The local tourist brochures call it "Number One Grand Spectacle on Earth".

The Stone Forest covers about 26,000 hectares (64,000 acres) of Yunnan Province, but most tourists confine themselves to a manageable area of concentrated wonders. Here they've paved the paths and built protective railings, but you could lose your way without a guide.

Near the starting point, women from the neighbouring village—members of the Sani tribe of the Yi nationality—sell embroidered blouses, bags and assorted knick-knacks. As you might imagine, the Stone Forest has a special mystical meaning for the indigenous people.

In an open area beyond a grove of giant bamboo, Chinese tourists hire native garb to have their pictures taken on horseback. To prove they were here, they pose in front of a stone wall carved with the simple Chinese characters for Shi Lin (Stone Forest).

Guides point out the formations resembling specific animals, plants and buildings. One pinnacle is even suspected of looking like Napoleon's silhouette. You'll be invited to squeeze through the **Narrowest Pass** between the rocks; Sani legend says it will add ten years to your life. From the highest point in the Stone Forest, **Peak Viewing Pavilion,** you get a comprehensive view of this great thicket of jagged rocks thrusting skywards.

The biggest open space in the Stone Forest, a lawn surrounded by cherry trees, is the site of a Sani festival each June. For 48 hours

Wind and water have shaped the fantastic limestone rocks of the Stone Forest.

non-stop the tribesmen devote themselves to singing and dancing, wrestling matches, bullfights (water-buffalo fighting each other), feasting and romancing.

Many of the celebrants come from **Five Trees Village** (*Wu Ke Shu*), across the lake from the hotel and tourist zone. This community of several thousand Sani also shelters countless water-buffalo, pigs, goats and dogs (some dangerous). In consideration for the sensibilities of the inhabitants, it's best not to stray from the main street unless you have a guide — or an invitation from one of the local people. The village consists of thatched-roof, mud-and-wattle houses. A ramshackle air pervades the place, but along the lake are small rice paddies which afford altogether inspiring views.

Tourists who stay the night are usually entertained with a Sani folklore show. The musicians and dancers have been threshing wheat or planting rice all day, so you must give them credit for unbounded energy. Among the instruments in the orchestra are flute, piccolo and zither, a giant banjo with a hollow bottom and a form of xylophone. The female dancers wear big conical red, white and black hats, while the men sport floppy black turbans. In song and mime they recount the legends that link their people to the eternal mysteries of the Stone Forest.

LANZHOU 兰州
(*Lanchow*)

Two legendary thoroughfares pass through Lanzhou — the broad, powerful Yellow River and the ancient trade route known as the Silk Road. Today the big, busy city boasts broad new boulevards as well as intriguing old streets of shops and houses. Adding colour, members of minority nationalities — mostly Muslim Hui people and Tibetans — contribute their own customs, costumes and cuisine. In some neighbourhoods the pavements are crowded with "free market" pedlars and artisans.

Lanzhou is the capital of Gansu (Kansu) Province, which extends from the farmland of the Yellow River basin through the narrow Gansu corridor with its steep rocky mountains to China's far west of desert and oases.

Lanzhou got its name under the Sui Dynasty more than a thousand years ago. In recent times its role as a transport centre has strengthened with the spread of the railways and air routes. Industrial development since 1949 has transformed the city, adding vast new suburbs of oil refineries and factories. The population of the metropolitan area now reaches 2 million.

The **Gansu Provincial Museum,** across the street from the big Soviet-style Friendship Hotel, houses perhaps the most famous

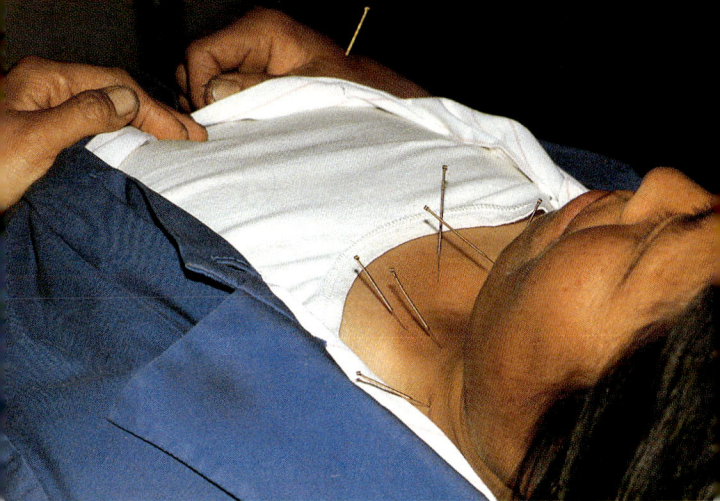

Doctors use acupuncture to cure ailments the traditional way.

sculpture in all of China: the galloping **"Flying Horse of Gansu"**, its right rear leg touching a symbolic bird, is the subject of countless reproductions at home and abroad. The original bronze was found in an ancient Han-Dynasty tomb in Gansu Province in 1969. You can buy a bronze copy in the museum shop—for a tidy sum.

From the same era, a 90-piece **bronze army** (one-tenth life size), of authoritative lancers riding to battle in chariots pulled by eager horses, is kept under glass on the museum's third floor. Also from the Han Dynasty two thousand years ago come bamboo strips inscribed with imperial edicts, medical prescriptions and miscellaneous records, plus figures carved of wood portraying various animals: a bull, geese and dogs—and a unicorn. (You'll appreciate the museum much more if you're accompanied by a competent local guide; the written explanations on the exhibits are in Chinese only.)

For a view of the muddy, swiftly moving Yellow River, and the city along its banks, go to **White Pagoda Hill Park** *(Bai Ta Shan Gongyuan)*, once a military stronghold. The temple itself, an octagonal seven-storey structure, was rebuilt in the 15th century.

Five Springs Hill Park *(Wu Quan Shan Gongyuan)* climbs a steep mountainside on the opposite bank of the river. The springs in question provide water for specialized needs, from making tea to ensuring fertility. To break up the climb there are temples and pavilions to visit and a big pond crossed by a zigzag bridge.

LESHAN 乐山

From the provincial capital of Chengdu it's a drive of more than three hours through populous Sichuan (Szechuan) Province to the town of Leshan, the base for visits to one of China's four "holy mountains".

A 13th-century poet wrote that the most beautiful scenery of China is found in Sichuan, and the best scenery of Sichuan is

concentrated in Leshan. Here, three rivers converge and flow along the city wall, and far away in the mist rises Mount Emei.

Boats ferry visitors from Leshan to the site of the **Great Buddha;** the trip takes only a few minutes. Whether seen from the river or, later, from the hillsides, this is an impressive spectacle — said to be the world's largest seated Buddha statue. Carved from the cliffside more than a thousand years ago, it measures 71 metres (233 feet) high. The statue's feet are so big that a hundred people can sit on each instep.

From the boat landing, 350 steps lead up to Ling Yun Temple. A bouncy suspension footbridge leads to a vantage point for a close-up look, out and down, onto the Great Buddha; you can even see the grass sprouting from the statue's shoulders and arms.

The lush subtropical scenery here is an attraction in itself. And then there are the teahouses situated in temples. The local people drink their tea from bowls, keeping a small saucer of hot water handy to replenish the brew.

Mount Emei 峨眉山

Dubbed "the fairest mountain among the fair mountains of the world," Mount Emei reaches an altitude of more than 3,000 metres (over 9,800 feet). You don't have to climb all the way to the summit to appreciate the mountain's charm and mystique. But the higher you go the more chance you'll have of sighting the rich fauna of the hill forests, from gregarious monkeys to the red panda.

The age of steam lives on in China.

The first stop on the way up Mount Emei is the 16th-century **Loyalty to Country Temple** *(Bao Guo Si)*, where an audio-visual show briefs tourists on the climb to come. After another couple of kilometres, the **Crouching Tiger Temple** *(Fu Hu Si)* features a small natural history museum, an art gallery almost wholly devoted to paintings of Mount Emei (all for sale), and a bronze pagoda.

There are monasteries and famous scenic spots every few kilometres of the way, but this is a climb for the energetic only. In any case, foreign tourists rarely have time to go beyond the first temples. Chinese tourists equip themselves with black bamboo walking sticks, sold here as souvenirs.

One curiosity of recent history is found on the slopes of Mount Emei. The **Hong Zhu Shan Hotel,** composed of several wooden buildings amid tall old trees, was for a time during World War II the headquarters of Generalissimo Chiang Kai-shek. He lived and worked in Building 4, a single-storey yellow building now reserved for foreign tourists. It was a long way from the pressures of war — no shellbursts could be heard, only the sound of the cicadas night and day.

Leshan's colossus of a Buddha is one of the largest in the world.

131

LUOYANG 洛阳
(Loyang)

The population of Luoyang is nearly a million—almost the same as it was during the Sui Dynasty 1,400 years ago. Those were the days of imperial glory. Luoyang is sometimes known as the Capital for Nine Dynasties, a political and cultural prominence that began nearly 4,000 years ago.

The long downward slide, preceded by many wars and disasters, began in the 10th century when China's imperial court moved to the north-east. Even so, Luoyang had the compensation of being capital of the central province of Henan. But by the 20th century it was only a shadow of its former self. After the Communists took power they decided to revive the small, sleepy city as a model industrial centre. Hundreds of new factories were built, turning out tractors, mining

The water-buffalo and wooden plough are familiar sights in rural China.

heyday — Shang bronzes and glazed Tang ceramic figures.

Workers' Park *(Laodong Renmin Gongyuan)*, formerly known as the Royal Town Park, was laid out more than 2,700 years ago. Two Han-Dynasty tombs have been unearthed here. Although the coffins have gone, the tombs and their mural paintings are important in themselves as examples of ancient architecture and art.

A few kilometres east of town, **White Horse Temple** *(Bai Ma Si)*, much restored over the ages, dates from the 1st century A.D. It was one of the first Buddhist monasteries built in China. The name refers to the legend that two monks from India who brought the first Buddhist scriptures to this place were mounted on white horses. These visitors are said to have been buried at the temple.

Long Men Caves 龙门石窟

Counted among the most precious grotto complexes in China, the Long Men Caves lie about 13 kilometres (8 miles) south of Luoyang. The name Long Men, which means Dragon's Gate, may derive from the lie of the land here; cliffs standing like gate tow-

equipment, ball bearings and thousands of other products.

Luoyang's most precious historical relics are to be found outside town. All the same the **Luoyang Museum,** housed in a Ming-Dynasty temple, provides a useful overall view of the city through the ages. Going back to the beginning, there is the fossil of an elephant tusk half a million years old. After Neolithic pottery and tools come finds from the city's ers rise on either side of the River Yi. Best time to visit is early morning when the rising sun lights up the contours of the statues, giving them an eerie, lifelike quality.

The hard rock was conducive to delicate carving, carried out on a monumental scale for about 400 years, starting in A.D. 494. Some statistics: more than 1,300 grottoes were constructed, as well as 2,100 niches and nearly 100,000 statues. These range from a height of 17 metres (56 feet) to a fingernail-sized 2 centimetres. By way of added attractions there are 40 pagodas and more than 3,600 inscribed steles or tablets, of keen interest to historians and calligraphers.

Some priceless sculpture was in the past looted by Europeans and Americans. Guides point to a wall from which two classic reliefs were chiselled in 1935 "by a Chinese curio dealer bribed by an American". The works ended up in museums in New York and Kansas City.

Among the earliest constructions, the three **Bin Yang Grottoes** were dedicated to the emperor and empress of the Northern Wei Dynasty (A.D. 386–534), after the capital was transferred to Luoyang. The principal sculpture, five times life-size, displays features typical of that dynasty's Buddhist art — a thin face, large eyes, straight nose and quiet smile.

The subtleties of Tang-Dynasty art may be seen in the **Qian Xi Temple,** begun in A.D. 641, and the **Feng Xian Temple,** constructed a few years later. The

Luoyang's Long Men Caves contain tens of thousands of sacred statues.

Feng Xian cave shelters a 17-metre (56-foot) Buddha, seated atop a thousand-petalled lotus and accompanied by lesser but equally brilliant statues of his disciples. The fierce heavenly guard trampling a devil underfoot is thought to bring good luck to those who put their arms around his ankle.

One of the oldest and most beautiful of the grottoes is **Gu Yang,** begun in A.D. 495 and completed under the Northern Qi in A.D. 575. The Buddha here is guarded by two magnificent lions at his feet.

A great curiosity of the complex, not at all sculptural, is the **Grotto of Prescriptions,** begun in A.D. 575. Inscriptions here amount to a compendium of ancient Chinese illnesses and treatments.

NANJING 南京
(Nanking)

This ancient capital of China has suffered so many catastrophes that few historic monuments have survived — and these are widely dispersed. Perhaps this is why much emphasis is placed on modern triumphs—the heroic bridge across the Yangtze River and the tallest building in the country.

But past and present are often juxtaposed in Nanjing, like the blue pedicabs sharing the streets with big new buses—or the fresh pink and white plum blossoms on the hillsides around the Ming tombs. On the far side of the famous bridge, a tranquil scene is revealed: ample fields of wheat, within sight of the bustling city.

Nanjing lies about 300 kilometres (185 miles) west of Shanghai in Jiangsu (Kiangsu) Province. Here the great Yangtze River narrows to slightly more than one kilometre, so even before there was a bridge the city held high strategic significance. Visitors are usually advised to avoid Nanjing in July and August, when the heat can become debilitating — temperatures of 40° C (above 100° F) are no rarity. But air conditioning is.

Nanjing means "Southern Capital", a name conferred rather late in the city's history. During its early grandeur under the State of Chu, the town was called Jin-ling, a name still used in literary and other allusions. Then in the 3rd century, in the era of the Three Kingdoms, it was christened Jianye. Under that or similar titles it served as the capital of six southern dynasties. The Ming emperors made it the national capital. The name Nanjing, in fact, was devised after the capital was moved north to Beijing in the 15th century.

In the 20th century a series of dramas overtook Nanjing. It was here that Dr. Sun Yat-sen was elected president of the republic. Chiang Kai-shek made it his capital until the advance of Japanese invasion forces induced him to head west. When the Japanese troops finally arrived in 1938, the "Rape of Nanking" was added to the catalogue of war's atrocities. (But no monument commemorates the victims, among whom perhaps 100,000 died in the first four days.) The Nationalists regained the battered city after the Japanese surrender in 1945. The Communist army crossed the Yangtze (which the Chinese call the Changjiang, or Long River) in April, 1949, bringing the new order to the old capital.

The **Yangtze River Bridge** is more than a significant engineering achievement. (Only three

A barber sets up shop in a quiet alleyway.

137

bridges span the entire river, and this one is the longest — 1,577 metres over water; a little less than a mile.) Proudly claimed to be the world's biggest two-tier bridge for rail and road traffic, it has greatly improved contacts between North and South China. And it inspired national self-confidence at the time of the Sino-Soviet schism of 1960. When the Soviet Union withdrew its technical experts, the Chinese built it themselves, in eight years.

Right in the centre of the city is a more recent landmark, a rare Chinese skyscraper—a 37-storey hotel. The **Jinling Hotel,** catering to foreign tourists, was a co-operative effort involving architects, engineers and operational experts from Hong Kong and overseas. Among other features considered revolutionary in China, it has a revolving roof restaurant with a helipad on top, and a six-level subterranean garage.

Nanjing claims a little-known distinction—the longest **city wall** in the world. In the 14th century, the Ming rulers mobilized 200,000 workers to build fortifications extending 33½ kilometres (nearly 21 miles). The largest of 24 city gates, newly renovated as a tourist attraction, is the **Zhong Hua Men,** on the southern edge of Nanjing. It was a formidable redoubt, with tunnels enough for 3,000 besieged defenders.

Rain Flower Terrace *(Yu Hua Tai),* just outside the south gate, mixes romance and tragedy. In the 6th century, according to legend, a certain Buddhist monk preached on this spot. The gods were so moved that blossoms wafted down from heaven. The tragedy is that this terrain was used as an execution ground in 1927, when the Kuomintang established power in Nanjing. A cemetery and Revolutionary

Spanning the Yangtze at Nanjing, the world's longest two-tiered bridge for road and rail traffic links North and South China.

Martyrs' Park have since been established. One curiosity here: the park is full of smooth, sparkling pebbles, popular with Chinese collectors, who put them in water to bring out the colours; souvenir shops sell them.

Also in southern Nanjing, the former **Palace of the Heavenly King** *(Tian Wang Fu)*, built when the forces of the Taiping Rebellion captured the city, now serves as headquarters of the Jiangsu provincial government. It was the most ambitious architectural project of the era (mid-19th century). The **Western Garden** is full of fine touches: an imaginative rock garden, a dragon wall, a children's maze and a bottle-shaped lake for an imperial stone houseboat.

The **Nanjing Museum,** founded in 1933, is located inside Zhong Shan Gate, the main eastern portal of the city wall. Among art and artefacts from prehistoric times to the end of the empire, the museum displays colourful ancient pottery, elegant figurines and a famous jade burial suit 2,000 years old.

Back in town, the Ming-Dynasty **Drum Tower** *(Gu Lou)* has been restored to its eminence on a hill in the very centre of Nanjing. The drum in question (since replaced) told the time and warned the citizens of danger. Now there's a tearoom upstairs and a viewing deck; souvenirs and works of art are on sale to tourists.

Nanjing's distinguished history as a political and cultural centre accounts for a considerable local pride. One achievement much vaunted here is the mass planting of trees, which at last report covered nearly one-third of the entire area of the city. (Beijing, by contrast, is said to have less greenery per inhabitant than any other world capital.) One area in which rivalry is freely revealed is the realm of cooking. Nanjing claims its salted duck is superior to the more famous Peking duck. Nanjing ducks, it's pointed out, are raised naturally on ponds, not force-fed like their less fortunate Beijing competitors.

Around Nanjing

Chinese pilgrims of all political persuasions come from many countries to the **Mausoleum of Dr. Sun Yat-sen,** the founder of the Chinese Republic, in the Purple Hills east of Nanjing. The blue-tile-roofed hillside complex could scarcely be more grandiose. You follow a long winding avenue planted with plane trees and continue up the 392 granite steps of the ceremonial staircase to the actual memorial hall. There are statues of Dr. Sun standing, sitting (by a French sculptor, Paul Landowski), and recumbent above the vault itself. On the ceiling is a mosaic version of the Kuomintang flag, a white star on a blue background. Dr. Sun often roamed these hills during his Nanjing years. It was his own wish that he be buried here, though he could never have anticipated the imperial splendour which developed.

Nearby in the Purple Hills is **Xiao Ling,** the tomb of Emperor

A major centre of pilgrimage, Nanjing's Mausoleum of Sun Yat-sen honours the founder of modern China.

Hong Wu, founder of the Ming Dynasty. What with wars and revolutions, not much is left of the 14th-century complex. But don't miss the **Sacred Way** lined with big stone statues of elephants, camels, horses, lions and mythical animals, which turns north into an approach road guarded by statues of generals and manda-

[...] in the hall above the burial site are displayed pictures of the emperor. Guides report he was even uglier in real life; two court artists are said to have lost their heads for an excess of realism in their portraits.

North-east of Nanjing, another major scenic area surrounds **Qi Xia Mountain** — which one Qing emperor called the "brightest and most beautiful mountain in Jin-ling". **Qi Xia Temple,** a complex of pavilions and halls, was begun in the 5th century. Housed here is a large Buddhist school, still in operation. Near the rear exit of the temple stands a five-storey, octagonal **stupa**, or shrine, more than a thousand years old. Incidents from the life of the Buddha are sculpted all around its stone base.

Beyond this, the **Thousand Buddha Cliff** is of sandstone, notoriously vulnerable to erosion. These grottoes may have been begun about 1,500 years ago, but they've needed renovations over the centuries. There are 515 statues in the several hundred grottoes that riddle the cliffside.

NANNING 南宁

The name of Nanning, but not much else about it, is easily confused with Nanjing (Nanking). Nanning (meaning "Tranquillity of the South") is the capital of the Guangxi Zhuang Autonomous Region, a stronghold of China's minority nationalities. Located south of the Tropic of Cancer, this river port is the nation's southernmost big city (population above half a million). The

average year-round temperature is a balmy 22° C (72° F), and flowers are always in bloom. Pineapples, lichees and mangoes grow here.

Minority ethnic groups are as much an attraction as the lush scenery. Nanning is the home of the Zhuang nationality, the biggest of China's minorities, and there are Miao, Yao, Yi and others — each with its own costumes and traditions. There are

Buddhism has its adepts—but they're mostly of the older generation.

so many tribes that in 1952 the Guangxi Institute for Nationalities was established on the western outskirts. Close to 2,000 students of a dozen ethnic groups study everything from politics to

143

science on the way to becoming functionaries and teachers.

But a thoroughly Chinese festival is the city's most famous folkloric attraction — the annual Dragon Boat Race on the fifth day of the fifth lunar month. Long, low boats with dragon prows are rowed at full splashing speed by crews vying for honour and the prize of a roast pig and wine. The race commemorates the poet-statesman Qu Yuan (Chu Yuan), who is said to have drowned himself in 295 B.C. over a matter of political honour.

Eight kilometres (5 miles) east of Nanning, the **Guangxi Botanical Garden of Medicine** is a pretty place to learn about Chinese traditional medicine. Thousands of different medicinal herbs are grown here, under scientific but fragrant conditions. They find their way into such products as a rheumatism medicine, a cough syrup, and Guangxi Sweet Tea, the leaves of which purportedly contain 300 times the sweetness of sugar cane.

A natural attraction 32 kilometres (20 miles) north of Nanning, the million-year-old **Yiling Cave,** has been open to the public

only since 1975. Admirers of stalactites and stalagmites can let their imaginations lead the way through caverns with "halls" as high as a ten-storey house. The walk-through — just over a kilometre — takes about one and a half hours. Since the temperature in the cave never fluctuates from a cool 18° C (64° F) year-round, visitors in summer are urged to take along a sweater.

The seaside town of Qingdao boasts sandy beaches, a promenade and pier.

QINGDAO 青岛
(Tsingtao)

Imagine Copacabana beach set down on the shore of the Yellow Sea and backed by pinewoods, parks and tree-shaded streets. The world-class resort setting is one of the surprises of Qingdao, an important seaport on the Shandong (Shantung) Peninsula.

Six beaches make this charming city one of China's favourite summer retreats. The sea is refreshing and so, usually, is the air, cooled in summer by the northerly ocean currents. Whether or not you join the Chinese masses and take the plunge, you'll appreciate the chance to see them at ease—sunbathing, strolling, having their pictures taken, eating ice-cream or dumplings.

As you might deduce from the Victorian architecture of the rail-

way station and many other buildings, Qingdao has an unusual history by any standard. Until the end of the 19th century, there was little here apart from fishermen's houses and a minor Chinese naval base. When Germany entered the imperialist age under Kaiser Wilhelm, Qingdao was selected as a likely port for development. A 99-year lease was imposed on the Manchu government.

Soon a modern, German-style city was built, with villas, a deep-water port, a cathedral and a main street named Kaiser-Wilhelm-Strasse. Business was not everything; the Germans used Qingdao as a missionary base. It remains one of China's rare Christian strongholds, where the twin-spired cathedral tends to be crowded with the local people on Sundays.

German Qingdao suffered a curious fate during World War I. Japan, which joined with the Allied forces, invaded the city, imprisoned the survivors of the German garrison and occupied Qingdao for the duration of the war. China wasn't able to regain sovereignty until 1922. After the Communists came to power in 1949 industrial development went forward. Even though the population now exceeds 4 million (including outlying regions), Qingdao keeps its quiet allure.

As permanent as any of the German contributions to Qingdao is the brewing prowess that proudly prevails. The hearty local beer is exported in big green bottles or modern cans under the old spelling of the town's name, Tsingtao.

Qian Hai Pier used to be the main berth for German ships. Now the pier has been lengthened to an impressive 110 metres (nearly a quarter of a mile); an octagonal pavilion lies at the far end. Holiday-makers mill about the promenade, and professional street photographers do business posing them with the lighthouse as background.

Overlooking the sea is the local **aquarium,** said to be the oldest in China, containing 60 big glass tanks of fish and other sea life. The neighbouring **Marine Products Museum** features bottled exhibits. Between the two institutions are pools occupied by sea lions and turtles. Offshore, sailing dinghies of the Qingdao Navigation Club, the first of its kind in China, are put through their paces.

About 30 kilometres (nearly 20 miles) east of Qingdao, the scenic mountain of **Laoshan** is famous for its legends and waterfalls. Laoshan mineral water, of vaunted medicinal value, is bottled at the source and sold everywhere in China. It also serves as a key ingredient of Qingdao's tasty beer.

SHANGHAI 上海

You couldn't confuse Shanghai with any other Chinese city. It is bigger, more prosperous, more dynamic than any other; its skyline boasts European-style towers; its shop windows and food stalls seize your attention. Before war and revolution changed the face of the city, Shanghai was dominated by foreign fortune-hunters, social climbers and a glittering array of sinners. Its very name became a transitive verb in English: to "shanghai", meaning to abduct by trickery or force. Nowadays visitors have nothing to worry about: wandering through the most obscure backstreets by day or night is perfectly safe. And always fascinating.

Shanghai's overall population, close to 12 million, makes it one of the two or three most extensive cities in the world, depending on how you count. For Shanghai covers a metropolitan area of about 6,000 square kilometres (more than 2,300 square miles)—five times the size of the city of Los Angeles. Administered as a separate region, like Beijing, the Shanghai metropolis includes rich farmland, as well as big-city housing complexes and heavy industry.

Shanghai's present position as a great industrial centre is not traditional. Rather, it was achieved by the Communist authorities in reaction to the city's history of conspicuous consumption. So today about 10,000 factories pour forth a pall of choking gas and smoke, which the government is striving to clear up. But Shanghai still has a special appeal to visitors as a sophisticated, businesslike metropolis — all the more colourful for its nostalgic associations.

Shanghai in History

China's prime port began unpromisingly a thousand years ago as a fishing village on mud flats near the Yangtze River's outlet to the East China Sea. Shanghai didn't officially become a town until the 13th century; even then it was largely ignored by the rest of China and the world.

During the 17th and 18th centuries, domestic commerce increased the importance of the town as a port and marketplace. But the authorities firmly resisted foreign connections — until British gunboats won an invitation After the first Opium War, Shanghai became one of five Chinese ports open to foreign residence and trade.

Over the next few years the influx of Europeans and Americans, as well as refugees from battles of the Taiping Rebellion, turned Shanghai into a glamorous, if naughty, boom town. But little of the prosperity filtered down to the ordinary citizen, who was kept apart. Bitterness at the injustices and corruption of Shanghai society fired the city's revolutionary movement: the Chinese Communist Party was founded here in 1921.

Shanghai was occupied by Japanese troops between 1937 and 1945; most of the foreign colony was interned. After the war the Kuomintang took power, but Communist troops seized Shanghai in 1949. The new regime wiped out organized crime and vice, expropriated factories and built new ones, setting the city on a new industrial course. In 1965 the Cultural Revolution was sparked off in Shanghai, the political base of Jiang Qing, the former Shanghai actress who was Mao's wife. After the death of Mao and the arrest of the Gang of Four, Shanghai culture and art experienced a renaissance.

Sightseeing

As an essentially 19th-century phenomenon, Shanghai matured too late to contribute to classical Chinese art or culture. If historic monuments are relatively rare, it doesn't mean the city lacks for sights. In Shanghai the interest shifts to relics of uninhibited pre-war capitalism and scenes of the city's contemporary energy and flair.

The **port** of Shanghai sums up the strange, often uncomfortable, meeting of East and West, of old and new. The muddy Huangpu River slices through the centre of the city, after passing interminable industrial suburbs with their

In Shanghai the consumer age is in—from plastic bottles to the latest in transport trucks.

fuming smokestacks. Foghorns converse into the night, long after the car horns and bike bells have ceased.

The river traffic is a motley flotilla of modern container ships and ocean-going junks, their sails the colour of grime, of packed ferries and convoys of barges, warships, rusty coasters and bobbing sampans. And then, in the almost inevitable haze, you see an astonishingly un-Chinese skyline, a mythical European metropolis transplanted.

The riverfront promenade on the left bank of the Huangpu used to be called the **Bund,** from an Anglo-Indian word for an embankment on a muddy shore. It's easy to imagine the elegance of the Bund in its heyday, when the gardens were barred to dogs and Chinese, in that order. This is the place for relaxed people-watching, from early morning when the shadow-boxers work out to the evening strolls of well-dressed courting couples.

Facing the river along Zhongshan Road are some of the grandiose old buildings, a bit the worse for wear: the **Peace Hotel,** formerly the elegant Cathay (where Noel Coward finished writing *Private Lives*), the **Seamen's Club,** formerly the British consulate, and the massive **City Hall,** built as the headquarters of the Hong Kong and Shanghai Bank.

Shanghai has more motor vehicles than any other Chinese city, so the streets echo with the hooting of truck horns and trolley buses, as well as with the bells of all the bikes (of which 4 million per year are manufactured in the city.) The decibel level stays far too high for comfort all day long. But the central business district is still a highlight for the sightseer, full of revelations about life in Shanghai.

The most famous and animated street of all, **Nanjing Road,** is lined with shops and stores reflecting Shanghai's remarkable standard of living, far higher than the national average. (Notice the businessmen in suits and ties and women carefully coiffed.) Traffic is so intense here that bicycles are banned; it's a modified pedestrian precinct in which cars are kept to the very middle of the road.

The establishments taken over from the capitalists after 1949 have new names like "No. 1 Department Store" and "Shanghai Food Store", the latter staffed by 1,000 employees. Nanjing Road reveals the whole range of Chinese consumer goods, often appealingly displayed. (But chic local shoppers prefer Huaihai Road, farther south.)

A junk in full sail cruises Shanghai's Huangpu River.

People's Park *(Renmin Gong-yuan)*, on the south side of Nanjing Road, used to feature a race-course, but gambling is sternly condemned in the People's Republic. Now the only runners are the local children, playing among the park's trees, ponds and lawns.

Tang-Dynasty figures on display in the Shanghai Museum.

Shanghai Museum 上海博物馆
In 1952 a former bank building was requisitioned to house the headquarters of a new museum. Today the **Shanghai Museum of Art and History** contains more than 200,000 items. The collection is divided into three main sections, one to a floor.

At the top, the Chinese Paintings Exhibition begins with Neolithic pottery and continues

through classic scroll paintings; Chinese artists had evolved a national style as early as the 4th century B.C. The stages in the development of Chinese calligraphy are also documented.

The Chinese Ceramics Exhibition, below, starts with 7,000-year-old pottery and includes life-sized terracotta figures from the 3rd century B.C., excavated at Xi'an in 1974. You may not become an expert, but you will appreciate the grace and originality of Chinese ceramics from Han-Dynasty pots to sophisticated 19th-century porcelain.

The first floor is devoted to Chinese bronzes, almost any one of which would be a major attraction in a museum in Europe or America. Works from the Shang and Zhou dynasties, dating back as far as 3,500 years, have never been surpassed. Their shapes, the method of casting, and of course the decorations and calligraphy, reveal important details about life in ancient China.

Other Sights

The **Yu Yuan Garden,** commissioned by a Ming-Dynasty mandarin, is the only classical Chinese garden in Shanghai. It is an absolute gem of landscaping and architecture, the perfect place for the local people to seek tranquillity, so conveniently offered in the heart of old Shanghai.

Just inside the main gate is a rockery, an artificial hill of inherently interesting stones, held together with glutinous rice powder and lime. From the pavilion atop this hill, the Ming official could watch all the excitements of river life, though tall buildings now intervene. In front of the Hall of Ten Thousand Flowers (not, of course, to be taken literally) grows a 400-year-old gingko tree. Another carefully created rockpile is reflected in a pond teeming with giant goldfish. All the corridors and pavilions, bridges and walls, sculptures and trees are so artfully arranged that the garden seems many times larger than its actual, compact area.

Outside the garden walls, a large rectangular pond is bisected by the **Nine-Zigzag Bridge,** so shaped to baffle evil spirits. This links to shore a 400-year-old **teahouse** with upswept roofs, a favourite place for the locals to take tea and cakes.

The teahouse pond marks one corner of the **Old Chinese City,** once deemed a danger zone for European visitors. You might still get lost in this maze of backstreets, reminiscent of a North African souk, but you couldn't come to any harm. Although it's all been tidied up, the Old City remains a fascinating assembly of tenements and market stalls selling fresh produce and snacks and trinkets; here you can buy a statue of Beethoven or the Venus de

Milo—just the souvenir of Shanghai you hadn't thought of.

West of the Old City is a landmark of modern history: the low brick building where the Chinese Communist Party was founded in July, 1921. This was in the French concession area, and when the French police learned of the clandestine meeting they raided the two-storey corner house. But they arrived too late to find the 12 conspirators, who included Mao Zedong. The Communist founding-fathers continued their congress aboard a hired excursion boat on a lake.

Another historical **museum,** on the opposite side of Fuxing Park, is the one-time home of Dr. Sun Yat-sen, honoured by Chinese of all ideologies as the founder of the modern nation. All the furniture is authentic, and the walls are crowded with historical photos documenting Dr. Sun's revolutionary career.

The 19th-century **Jade Buddha Temple** *(Yu Fo Si)*, in north-west Shanghai, houses two priceless jade Buddha statues, one in the seated position of enlightenment, the other reclining. Most statues in Buddhist temples are moulded of clay with a thin overlay of gold, so these giant jade works attract curiosity-seekers as well as wor-

China's keep-fit enthusiasts swear by tai chi.

shippers. Around the back of the altar is a flamboyant three-dimensional mural. An extra attraction for tourists: there's an antique shop in the compound, with some unusual items at interesting prices.

Shanghai's only ancient pagoda, part of the **Long Hua Temple** complex in the south-west suburbs, was rebuilt more than a thousand years ago. The seven-storey, octagonal structure was restored in the 1950s. But no one tried to correct its appealing tilt—insignificant when compared to the Tower of Pisa but notable nonetheless. Tiny bells, suspended from the corners of the upswept eaves, tinkle in the breeze.

An architectural monument of another kind altogether, again in the city, is the **Industrial Exhibition Hall,** originally titled the Palace of Sino-Soviet Friendship. Spired if uninspired, this huge building was a gift from the Soviet Union in the 1950s; it would have looked more at home in Stalin-era Moscow. One wing of the hall houses the Shanghai Arts and Crafts Fair, where foreign tourists can survey the output of local artisans.

Tourists are often taken to factories or workshops as well—for instance, the Shanghai Carpet Factory, where more than a thousand employees turn out carpets and tapestries. The Jade Carving Factory carries on a 3,000-year-old Chinese tradition. The amount of talent and effort invested in each item explains the considerable prices. At the Shanghai Arts and Crafts Research Studio, artisans may be observed as they carve ivory or bamboo, embroider, or cut intricate designs from paper. Here, too, a handicrafts shop is placed conveniently alongside.

Some tours take in the **Shanghai Zoo,** occupying the site of a former golf course in the western suburbs. Among the inhabitants are Chinese elephants, tigers, leopards and crocodiles—and of course giant pandas.

Much of Shanghai cuisine is based on vegetables; some favourite local dishes are based on beancurd, mushrooms and bamboo shoots. But the best known Shanghai recipes capitalize on the city's proximity to seafood. Steamed freshwater crabs, in season from October through to December, are the highlight of the year for many gourmets.

If you crave a change from Chinese food, Shanghai is probably the best place in China to abandon chopsticks. Thanks to the city's cosmopolitan history, European food is always available.

Country produce travels down the Grand Canal to market.

SUZHOU 苏州
(Soochow)

For centuries Suzhou has been famous for its canals and gardens, its beautiful women, and the musical cadences of the local dialect. (An old Chinese proverb, referring to the area's linguistic charms, says: Even an argument in Soochow sounds sweeter than flattery in Canton.)

Marco Polo found the inhabitants better traders than warriors and he described the city as large and magnificent. So much silk was produced, he reported, that every citizen was clothed in it, and the surplus exported. Even now silk retains its significance in the local economy.

Whether you go to Suzhou from Shanghai or Nanjing, you'll

Silken Secrets

When the Bombyx mori caterpillar is ready to turn into a moth, it exudes a single, continuous fibrous strand, hundreds of metres long, and wraps itself in a watertight cocoon. That caterpillar is the silkworm; the strand it spins is pure silk; and the secret of its cultivation has been known to the Chinese for 4,000 years.

Even as early as the 14th century B.C., silkworms were domesticated by Chinese farmers, who fed them on mulberry leaves and soaked the cocoons in warm water to free the silken yarn.

By the 1st century A.D. silk production was prospering to such an extent that a Chinese emperor was able to distribute a million rolls of silk cloth along the northern frontier to pacify marauders. Roman women craved the gossamer fabric exported to Europe along the old Silk Road, the legendary trade route across Central Asia to the Roman Empire.

The secret of silk manufacture was so jealously guarded that the penalty for revealing it was death by torture. Even so, the Roman Emperor Justinian, lamenting that so much money was being spent on silk, encouraged the smuggling of silkworms from China into Syria, where a new silk industry sprang up.

Nevertheless, the Chinese excelled in embroidered silk, patterned with dragons, birds and flowers; and Chinese damasks and brocades continued to be exported from China to Europe in the Middle Ages.

Today, 10 million Chinese farmers produce more than half the world's supply of silk fibre. The thread is wound off the cocoons almost by the kilometre, but it can take up to 1,000 cocoons to produce a single shirt.

Most luxurious of natural fibres, silk is also the most resilient, with a tensile strength greater than a filament of steel.

be moved by the wayside scenery, typical of China's "land of fish and rice". Sampans and scows ply the canals that divide the farmlands, where barefoot peasants in straw coolie hats squelch through the muddy rice fields. The Grand Canal is crowded with strings of barges laden with fruit and vegetables, construction materials or coal. Suzhou means "Plentiful Water".

The Grand Canal, second only to the Great Wall as a Chinese engineering achievement, was begun 2,400 years ago. By the 6th century A.D., it linked Suzhou and other rich farming areas of

Each cocoon yields reams of silken fibre.

This painting from the Ming era is on view in Jin Ci Temple park near Taiyuan.

the south with the consumers of the north — most notably the emperor and his court, who appreciated their fresh food regardless of the season. Canal excursions by tourist boat often begin in Suzhou, continuing to another enchanted city, Wuxi (see p. 177).

But Suzhou is best known for its perfectly landscaped, classical Chinese gardens. More than 150 were laid out, the first over a thousand years ago. The **Humble**

Administrator's Garden *(Zhuo Zheng Yuan)*, built by a Ming-Dynasty mandarin not otherwise remembered for humility, is the largest of all. As befits the city of Plentiful Water, ponds make up the better part of the terrain. And where there are ponds there are almost bound to be artificial islands, winding bridges, gazebos and weeping willows.

To the west, the **Tarrying Garden** *(Liu Yuan)* is a refuge of flowers and trees, courtyards and halls. This one, too, was built by a Ming civil servant as a place for meditation. While you linger, contemplate the 5-ton rock shipped here 400 years ago from Lake Tai because of its inspiring shape. Nearby **West Garden** *(Xi Yuan)* was given to a Buddhist monastery. The temple was destroyed in the Taiping Rebellion, then rebuilt.

Probably the smallest of all the Suzhou gardens, right in the centre of town, is the **Garden of the Master of the Nets** *(Wang Shi Yuan)*, covering half a hectare (barely more than an acre). The garden's founder, a retired politician, claimed he had given up public life to become a fisherman. Whatever his interests, he could hardly fail to be inspired by the view from his simple study.

Among Suzhou's touristic highlights, the highest is **Tiger Hill** *(Hu Qiu)*, a man-made hill built 2,500 years ago. It is rich in contrived rock formations and vegetation and waterfalls. From the summit rises a seven-storey brick **pagoda;** like the one in Shanghai, it leans from the vertical, but modern reinforcements should relieve your anxiety.

TAIYUAN 太原

If you go to Taiyuan by air, you'll be struck by the vast area of tortured terrain surrounding the fertile Taiyuan Basin: loess hillsides that look like architects' models of hills, naturally terraced but bleak.

Taiyuan is the capital of Shanxi (Shansi) Province, which you'll be lucky not to confuse with neighbouring Shaanxi (Shensi) Province. The city, with a history of more than two thousand years, now makes iron and steel, heavy machinery and fertilizer. The population is over a million.

The pre-eminent tourist attraction of Taiyuan, a group of temples called **Jin Ci**, lies 25 kilometres (16 miles) south-west of the city at the foot of Xuanweng Mountain. Jin Ci, thought to be more than one thousand years old, has an appealing combination of landscape and historic buildings—nearly a hundred pavilions, halls, terraces and bridges.

The most impressive of the temples, the **Temple of the Holy Mother** *(Sheng Mu Dian)*, was built in the Northern Song Dynasty. (The mother thus sanctified was the parent of Prince Shu Yu, himself much honoured in the Jin Ci complex.) The ancient wooden building, its ceiling supported without pillars, contains a seated statue of the prince's mother, surrounded by 43 life-sized statues of her ladies-in-waiting. Their faces, bearing and dress are all different — a treasured gallery of terracotta characters reflecting a real humanity rather than the customary Buddhist projections.

The most beautiful spot in the temple complex is the **Eternal Spring** *(Nan Lao Quan)*, the source of the Jinshui River. A great poet of the Tang Dynasty, inspired by the sight of the spring's crystal water, wrote, "Out of Jin Temple flows green jade". An octagonal pavilion stands next to the spring.

In Haozhuang village, a few kilometres south-east of Taiyuan, an unusual temple was built during the Ming Dynasty more than 400 years ago. **Twin Pagoda Monastery** *(Shuang Ta Si)* features two identical pagodas of 13 storeys each, about 30 metres (100 feet) apart. The twin pagodas have become Taiyuan's best known symbol. Alongside the pagodas stand more than 200 tablets inscribed in various styles of Chinese calligraphy.

The **Shanxi Provincial Museum** is divided into two sections, housed in two separate buildings in Taiyuan. The first, in a former Confucian temple, concentrates on politics and the evolution of the economy. The second, on the west side of May 1 Square, contains historic bronzes, ceramics, sculptures and paintings.

TIANJIN 天津
(Tientsin)

With its vital sea, air, road and rail connections, Tianjin is such an important transportation and industrial centre that it is ruled directly by the central government (as are Beijing and Shanghai). The population is more than 3 million.

Like Beijing, which is 120 kilometres (74 miles) to the northwest, Tianjin undergoes long, hard winters and brief but hot

---

Historical Footprints

You can still see them, though rarely now: old Chinese women hobbling along on deformed feet. They suffered no accident, no illness. They are living relics of the feudal practice of foot-binding.

As early as the Song Dynasty, nearly a thousand years ago, the notorious preference for women with small feet took a sinister turn. Small girls had their feet bandaged to prevent them from growing. The fact that they could never again walk normally seemed secondary to the potential appeal of "three-inch feet". After all, beautiful ladies had no reason to walk or work, anyway.

Foot-binding was outlawed from time to time but generally remained a fact of Chinese life over the centuries. It began to die out only after the fall of the monarchy in 1911.

summers. The rainy season comes in July and August. Autumn is considered the best time for a visit.

Tianjin has no major sites of historical interest. Although its development began under the Yuan Dynasty in the 14th century, it is mostly a contemporary city. Much of modern Tianjin, along with old landmarks, was damaged in the Tangshan earthquake of 1976, one of the worst natural disasters of our time.

Even so, you'll notice many European-style buildings in the city. These are relics of old Tientsin, the foreign concession port, opened to trade and settlement in 1858. In the city's heyday the major imperial powers, led by Britain, France and Japan, established flourishing enclaves here. The 500-year-old city wall was destroyed at the turn of the 20th century.

Foremost among the limited sightseeing possibilities in Tianjin is the **Park on the Water** *(Shui Shang Gongyuan)*, in the southwest district. Half of the park's area is water, so swimming, sailing and rowing are popular pastimes. There are 13 islets connected by all manner of graceful bridges. A four-storey pavilion on Islet No. 2 offers a view over the whole park.

Islet No. 9 is the site of the new Tianjin **Zoo.** Lions and tigers, bears and giraffes are on show, but the foreign tourists always rush to see the giant pandas. These cuddlesome black-and-white beasts spend most of their waking time eating. Each panda can consume 15 to 20 kilogrammes (33 to 44 pounds) of bamboo every day. The delicate leaves are the best part.

In 1978 a **memorial hall** to Zhou Enlai was opened in one building of Nankai Middle School, where the future prime minister studied as a teenager. His early academic and revolutionary activities are recorded in photographs and documents from 1913 to 1917.

Handicrafts are one of Tianjin's traditions, and tourists are sometimes taken to local arts and crafts factories, where such typical items as kites, painted clay figurines, and jade and ivory carvings are made. Groups also visit Tianjin's No. 1 Carpet Factory. Here high quality carpets in bright, permanent colours are created by hand. Workers also turn out small, easily portable carpets that tourists may buy to carry home.

Chinese gourmets at home and abroad know about Tianjin's favourite snack, steamed dumplings known as *goubuli* (more formally called Tianjin *baozi*). Only local cooks seem to know how to make them. Invented more than a hundred years ago by a Tianjin bun-shop owner, they have lately been exported to Japan.

TURPAN 吐鲁番
(Turfan)

The sidewalks of Turpan would turn to mud if it ever rained. But it almost never does. Here in the middle of the great desert in Xinjiang (Sinkiang) Autonomous Region, only 16 millimetres (little more than half an inch) of rain ever reaches the ground in an average year. Most evaporates on the way down.

Because of Turpan's location and climatic handicaps, it's startling to discover a sizeable city where houses are supplied with electricity and running water, and shady trees line the streets. It's an amazing oasis, a bastion of civilization in a climate as cruel as any on earth.

Turpan's secret is underground water, utilized today as it has been for thousands of years: a system

of interconnecting wells *(karez)* that relay mountain water underground to the oasis. (If the aqueduct were above ground, the water would almost all be lost by evaporation.) Throughout the region these tunnels, all dug by hand, stretch for perhaps 3,000 kilometres (more than 1,800 miles). Thanks to the *karez*, Turpan grows cotton, and melons and grapes of great sweetness and renown. And the desert is kept at bay by bountifully irrigated stands of elm, poplar and palm trees.

But the climate of China's "oven" remains hostile to humans. In the summer, when the

A heated platform serves as living, eating and sleeping quarters for this Muslim family of Turpan.

temperature exceeds 40°C (104°F) for days at a time, the locals take refuge in cellars until the night breeze comes up. In the springtime, when the mercury is merely in the 30s (close to 90°F), the people dress for a chill—the men in their long underwear, the women in thick brown stockings and gaily coloured headscarves.

Turpan is about 200 kilometres (125 miles) south-east of Urumqi, the regional capital. The trip is relentlessly downhill, for Turpan lies at the centre of the earth's deepest dry depression, dipping far below sea level. It's so dry and (except for winter) hot in the oasis that tourists are advised to drink as much tea or juice as possible to forestall dehydration.

Two thousand years ago the Silk Road traders stopped in Turpan for water and rest. The **bazaar** of today might give you the impression that little has changed:

Watermelons grow in the arid country round Turpan; Muslim arches frame the doorways of a home dug into the loess soil.

there are outdoor butcher shops, cobblers, dentists, a shooting gallery and merchants selling medicinal herbs, embroidered skullcaps, tobacco by the pocketful. Makeshift restaurants dish up spicy kebabs and the bread called *nang*. The customers, mostly of the Hui and Uygur nationalities, are as colourful as an oriental rug.

Aside from the thoroughly engrossing marketplace, the only formal sightseeing attraction within the town is a mosque with a graceful, 200-year-old **minaret,** variously known as Suleiman's Minaret or the Imin Pagoda. Unfortunately, two brick smokestacks of majestic stature loom large on the skyline, rather confusing the issue.

Of the major archaeological sites in the area, the nearest is the ancient city of **Jiaohe,** 13 kilometres (8 miles) west of Turpan. Founded in the 2nd century B.C., the city, like ancient Xi'an, was laid out in a grid. Jiaohe was destroyed at the end of the 14th century, but you can wander through the temple—the remaining walls provide a welcome bit of shade—and see the niches where statues of Buddha once stood. Guides point out the damaged earthen walls of what were once aristocratic homes, the wine factory, the jail.

Another ancient city, **Gaochang,** 46 kilometres (29 miles) east of Turpan, supported a population of 30,000. The imposing

Muslims of Turpan observe prayers in the local mosque.

city wall, with a perimeter of 5 kilometres (3 miles), is well preserved. Gaochang, which reached its prime during the Tang Dynasty, was destroyed in the 14th century, when Islam overtook Buddhism here. A sign at the entrance to the compound, in English, Chinese and Japanese, says belatedly: "Please don't take the relics of the ruins of the old city away".

An archaeological adventure awaits at the site of the **Astana Cemetery,** near Gaochang. Graves believed to be at least 1,500 years old were discovered by accident in 1972. Because of the almost total lack of moisture, the murals in the tombs have retained their lively colours. The site is so unspoiled that visitors are taken into the tombs by a local woman who owns the only flashlight (torch) within miles. The polychrome figurines unearthed here — impressions of dancing girls, a polo player and a camel are displayed at the museum in Urumqi.

Between Turpan and the eastern archaeological zones the road goes past **Flaming Mountain** (*Kizilatak* in Uygur). Facing south, the mountain attracts and stores the sun's heat; to sweltering passers-by the deep fissures might resemble flames. A temperature of 75°C (167°F) has been recorded here. Be glad you're not trudging through on the back of a donkey or camel.

URUMQI 乌鲁木齐市
(Urumchi)

In Mongolian, Urumqi means "Fine Pasture". In Uygur it's spelled with umlauts — Ürümqi. The Chinese make four syllables of it. However you read or write it, Urumqi is as exotic as its name.

The flight from Beijing to the capital of China's far-west region of Xinjiang takes more than three and a half hours; hardly time enough to ease the transition from the essential Chineseness of Beijing to the Central Asian tribal atmosphere of Urumqi.

All the signs and posters in Urumqi are bilingual, in Chinese and Uygur, the languages of the two largest nationality groups here. A dozen other ethnic minorities are represented in the city— mostly Kazakhs, Mongolians and Huis. This makes for some lively costumes and music as well as varied styles of food and drink.

The latest population figures put the Urumqi metropolitan area above the one million mark, and many new red-brick or prefabricated apartment houses line the wide tree-shaded avenues. But most people inhabit low traditional buildings painted yellow or light blue or both. There is an abundance of modest mosques.

And always in the background are the forceful mountains, usually as cheerless a sight as the surrounding desert. The distant peaks are covered with snow the year round. The city, though, is snowbound only from mid-November to March. The nicest time to visit is from May to September, when the flowers bloom and fruit trees offer up an abundant harvest.

The Xinjiang Uygur Autonomous Region, as the area is officially called, covers one-sixth of the total area of China. It borders the Soviet Union, Mongolia, Afghanistan, Pakistan and India, which accounts for the cosmopolitan look of Urumqi, an ancient Silk Road stopping place.

By way of sightseeing, no place is more fascinating than the local **bazaar,** a free market (of private entrepreneurs) selling fish, vegetables, clothing and sunglasses. Watchmakers, cobblers and restaurateurs all compete for custom. The market's irresistible kebabs, homemade noodles and round flat breads distract from the business at hand.

More formal, government-run shopping is concentrated in the main **department store** nearby. The customers are more colourful than most of the merchandise, but on the third floor a small department serves the special needs of the minority nationalities—bright textiles, jewellery, skullcaps, and butcher's knives.

Foreign tourists are usually taken to the **Minorities Exhibition,** actually a store where Xinjiang specialities are sold. There are local carpets in the Persian style, ornate skullcaps, deadly looking small knives in bronze scabbards and all manner of stringed instruments, mostly of the mandolin family. Xinjiang jade, which is white, is highly regarded.

Snow-capped peaks fringe the deserts of north-west China.

The **Xinjiang Museum,** in one of the province's most ostentatious buildings, is full of extremely interesting exhibits. Happily, most of the explanatory cards are in English as well as Chinese and Uygur, but the lighting is dim and the displays are unimaginative. Here you can see Stone-Age implements from the Turpan area; Han-Dynasty coins, fashionably narrow gold earrings, ornamented tiles and silk designs; and charming Tang-Dynasty figurines (also from Turpan tombs). Six mummies, embalmed as long ago as the 13th century B.C. but well preserved in the dry desert air, occupy a room of their own. Another wing mounts reproductions from the Thousand Buddha Grottoes of Kizil, at the foot of the Tianshan mountains in Xinjiang. The originals of these aston-

ishing murals, from the Han to the Tang dynasties, cannot yet be seen by tourists, but the copies here give a good idea of their impressive variety and beauty.

Three hours of difficult driving lead from Urumqi to **Heavenly Lake** *(Tian Chi)*, a placid mountain lake 1,950 metres (6,400 feet) above sea level. This trip is only possible between May and the end of September; the rest of the year the lake is frozen and the tortuous road impassable. But it must have been considerably more difficult when Wang Mu (Queen Mother) of the Western Zhou Dynasty (11th–8th centuries B.C.) visited the lake and gave a banquet for a local nomadic matriarch.

The road traverses a prairie-land that's all but uninhabited, except for an occasional shepherd and cowherd. At a higher altitude, rich grasslands parallel the rocky bed of a rushing river. Here are the yurts of the Kazakh cowboys. Then comes a gruelling climb on a gravel road up into a fragrant, scenic land of pine trees and mountain flowers. The cold, deep water of Heavenly Lake reflects the clouds, the trees and snow-capped peaks of the lofty mountains. Boat trips are organized for tourists in summer.

The hotpot simmers as a Mongolian family eat in their yurt.

WUHAN 武汉

A lively industrial and intellectual centre, Wuhan is equidistant from Beijing, Guangzhou, Shanghai and Chongqing. Its setting, at the confluence of the Yangtze and Han rivers, has made it a key traffic junction. The wail of river-boat foghorns mingles with the steam-engine whistles on the nation's main north-south railway.

The story of Wuhan has always been anchored in the vital, muddy Yangtze. So wide and treacherous is the river that before the great concrete-and-steel bridge of Wuhan was finished in 1957, all communications depended on ferries, often hampered by fog or flood. Now the two-tiered **Changjiang Bridge** (Yangtze River Bridge) is proudly shown to tourists as a triumph of the new China. So are the **dikes,** so tall they cut off the view of the river from the embankment. But the Yangtze's rages can't always be contained. In 1983 Wuhan was flooded in spite of monumental preparations for the worst.

Wuhan is a modern, composite name for three historic, contiguous cities: *Wu*chang, *Han*kou and *Han*yang. Wuchang, the oldest, is bountifully supplied with parklands. Hankou, on the opposite bank of the Yangtze, was opened

Wrestling is a traditional Mongolian sport.

to foreign development in the 19th century as a Treaty Port. (At high tide 10,000-ton ships can reach the harbour from the sea, some 1,500 kilometres [a thousand miles] away.) Hanyang, separated from Hankou by the Han River (requiring another, less heroic, bridge), is more typically Chinese.

After the Opium Wars, Hankou was carved up into British, French, German, Japanese and Russian zones of influence. In Zhongshan Avenue you can still make out the words "Poste Police", a relic of the French concession, inscribed on a wall; it's the only foreign sign remaining in Wuhan. But many of the old buildings in European style are left. The municipal office buildings on the embankment, administering a city which has grown beyond 4 million, are cast in the German mould.

But Wuhan, the capital of Hubei (Hupeh) Province, also has a significant revolutionary history. The rebellion of October 1911, inspired by Dr. Sun Yat-sen, began here—and Hankou suffered heavy damage in the fighting. The Central Peasant Movement Institute, where Communist activists were trained in the 1920s, was established in Wuchang. Mao Zedong taught here.

Hanyang's main historic landmark, **Gui Yuan Temple,** sprawls among pines and cypresses. Built about 400 years ago, it is the only one of Wuhan's 20 or more Buddhist temples not destroyed by Red Guards during the Cultural Revolution. Among its most precious possessions are 5th-century Tang sculptures and a white jade Buddha from Burma with a diamond in its forehead. The Hall of Five Hundred Disciples is a fascinating gallery of statues: grinning, yawning, frowning, meditating, leering —each one different.

The **Ancient Lute Terrace** *(Gu Qin Ta)* commemorates a 2,500-year-old legend of the deep friendship between a lute-playing mandarin and a music-loving woodcutter. Amateur musicians hold forth in the teahouse here, a favourite meeting place of local pensioners.

Across the mile-long Yangtze River Bridge in Wuchang is the **Yellow Crane Tower** *(Huang He Lou)*, predicated on another legend. First built in A.D. 223, the wooden structure burned down and was reconstructed several times. In 1981 the latest rebuilding project got under way about one kilometre from the original site. The design and decor of the new tower are based on paintings from the Yuan and Ming dynasties and a model of the Qing-Dynasty version.

East Lake *(Dong Hu)* is vaunted as the largest lake in any municipal park in China — 33 square kilometres (nearly 13 square miles) of invitingly clear water. Boating, swimming and fishing (tackle may be rented by the half-hour) are popular here. Of course, no Chinese lake would be complete without its artificial islands, causeways, pavilions and gazebos. Depending on the season—Wuhan is in the subtropical zone — the floral spectacle here might be peach and plum blossoms, orchids or osmanthus.

The **Hubei Provincial Museum,** near East Lake, owes its excellence to a chance discovery in 1978. The tomb of the Marquis Yi of the State of Zeng, 108 kilometres (67 miles) north-west of Wuhan, yielded treasure enough to furnish several museums. About 1,000 items—15 per cent of the total hoard — are now on display.

The Marquis, who lived in the 5th century B.C., died greatly mourned at the age of 25. He was buried together with his dog and 21 female sacrifices, plus tributes ranging from bronze wine vessels to enough musical instruments for an orchestra. The proudest musical exhibit is a set of 65 intricately decorated bronze bells, restored to their original resonance. Visitors hear a tape recording of the bells interpreting both Chinese and Western music; they sound like a cross between a glockenspiel and a modern carillon.

WUXI 无锡
(Wuhsi)

They ought to have chosen a more poetic name for this appealing town. Wuxi means "no more tin", a reference to the depletion, a couple of thousand years ago, of the local mines.

Wuxi is an industrial and marketing centre with a population of more than 800,000 in the "land of fish and rice", a fertile semi-tropical region. It lies 128 kilometres (80 miles) north-west of Shanghai —close enough for a hectic day trip by train. Canals and rivers crisscross the city, and the Grand Canal, one of the symbols of ancient China's advanced civili-

Public parks and workers' holiday homes edge the waters of Lake Tai.

The Grandest of Canals

The bustling boats and barges that throng the Grand Canal at Wuxi recall the days when this great waterway was China's main north-south artery. For more than 2,000 years, successive dynasties linked lakes and rivers across the eastern flatlands creating one single canal, 40 paces wide, from Hangzhou in the south, across the Yangtze and Yellow rivers to the old capital, Chang'an, and on to Beijing. Paved roads were built along each bank, shaded by elms and willows.

To celebrate the opening of the canal in A.D. 610, the emperor sailed along it in his four-decked imperial barge, escorted by a flotilla of dragon boats and followed by a retinue of eunuchs, concubines and officials. Temporary palaces and pavilions housed them at each halt.

In its heyday, some 15,000 junks, sampans and barges plied the water highway, carrying grain, timber, salt, fish, cloth and pottery, as well as luxury goods from the south.

With the advent of the railways and coastal steamers the canal lost its importance. Crops were often grown and houses built in the old canal bed. But today the Grand Canal is being restored and used once again as a means of transport, as well as to water the paddy-fields and control floods.

zation, flows right through the centre of town.

Even a short boat ride through the city on the **Grand Canal** produces unforgettable sights and photos; for sheer human interest it outdoes Venice. People line the bridges (each of a different design) to wave. Human-propelled ferryboats scurry out of the way. Long trains of barges, decks heaped with onions, reeds or bricks, la-

bour past. The riverside dwellers, whose quaint old houses were whitewashed at government expense in the interest of tourism, wash their clothes in the canal, and fish in it. You may even see a fisherman, assigning his captive cormorants to dive, their gullets collared to stop them eating the catch.

The Grand Canal project, begun 2,400 years ago, created an inland waterway stretching 1,794 kilometres (1,113 miles) from Beijing to Hangzhou. Canal excursions organized for foreign tourists range from a half-day tour to a seven-day cruise taking in Su-

Ancient houses with wooden balconies overlook the Grand Canal in Wuxi.

zhou, Wuxi, Changzhou, Zhenjiang, and the Yangtze River port of Yangzhou. The tourist authorities of Jiangsu Province also promote bicycle tours through the flat, green countryside.

Two lakes occupy half the total municipal area of Wuxi, compounding the atmosphere of waterside beauty. **Lake Tai** is a vast freshwater expanse boasting 72 islets. Boat trips on the lake go to Turtle Head Island *(Yuan Tou Zhu)*, a sanctuary of trees and flowers, bridges and pavilions. But more than any specific landfall, the lake is a spectacle on its own, with its fleet of fishing junks and roving sampans. The freshwater crabs from Lake Tai head the list of Wuxi gastronomic specialities.

Lake Li, connected to Lake Tai, is the setting for a famous garden, **Li Yuan.** The exemplary landscape reveals arched bridges, gaudy pavilions, covered promenades, open walkways, fish ponds and a miniature pagoda.

Another frequent stop for foreign tourists is a factory producing clay figurines—a 400-year-old Wuxi tradition. Also by way of industrial expeditions, there are visits to the local silk spinning and finishing plant. More shopping opportunities await at an antique store and, nearby, a street market where anyone who needs one can buy a live chicken, duck or snake.

XI'AN 西安
(Sian)

When ancient Peking was just a remote trading post, Xi'an was the capital of the Middle Kingdom and one of the world's biggest, richest cities. Palaces, pavilions and pagodas crowned the skyline. Artists and poets—and, of course, cooks—catered to the most demanding imperial tastes. And since this was the starting point of the Silk Road, the most outlandish foreigners congregated here.

Having made history over several thousand years, the city of today is more populous than ever and proud of its leafy new avenues, modern factories and housing projects. But there's no avoiding the past in this treasure house of Chinese civilization. Xi'an and its countryside hold the hoards of eleven dynasties.

On the way to any of the archaeological sites you get a good look at the strange, windwhipped land of the Wei River valley. Militarily and economically strategic since prehistoric times, the area comprises fertile cotton and wheat fields, fallow plains and bizarre terraces of loess—riddled with caves that provide alternative housing even to this day. The children here are almost theatrically applecheeked, not just from good health but from the stimulation of wind and dust storms.

Now the capital of Shaanxi Province, Xi'an can look back almost with detachment on its regal past. During the first Zhou Dynasty (which ended in 770 B.C.) several places in the Xi'an district served as capitals. In the 3rd century B.C., the Qin settled just north-west of Xi'an, in Xian-yang. When the Han took over, in 206 B.C., a grandiose new capital called Chang'an (Everlasting Peace) rose just north of Xi'an. Imperial splendour returned under the Sui (A.D. 581–618) when a capital called Daxing (Great Prosperity) was established on the site of Xi'an. The Tang emperors who followed greatly enlarged and beautified the city, again named Chang'an.

The golden age of Chang'an/Xi'an ended more than a thousand years ago when the Tangs succumbed to rebellion and anarchy. The city sank into provinciality, even though impressive new city walls and official buildings were constructed in the 14th century. These features of the Ming era—almost modern by Xi'an standards—are the first to catch the eye.

Sightseeing

The rectangular **city wall** of Xi'an is nearly 14 kilometres (more than 8 miles) long, and so thick that two-way chariot traffic could move along the roadway on top. A major renovation programme is under way to repair the ramparts, beautify the moat, and provide gardens and lawns.

Also from the Ming Dynasty, the **Bell Tower** *(Zhong Lou)* is another of those lofty wooden buildings ingeniously constructed without the use of nails. Three storeys of elegantly eaved roofs rise from a solid brick pedestal. As the centre of the city moved, over the centuries, so did the Bell Tower, which reached its present site in the 16th century. It was restored in 1740 and again in modern times.

The **Drum Tower** *(Gu Lou)*, a similar building though not quite as tall, dates from 1370. Drums were beaten to signal the night curfew and, in the morning, the reopening of the city gates. The age of tourism has caught up with this landmark: upstairs they've opened a big antique shop for foreigners.

Around the corner, the **Great Mosque** *(Qing Zhen Si)* traces its history to the 8th century, though it has been rebuilt a number of times. Were it not for the Arabic inscriptions you might not guess that this is a mosque, for the spacious complex consists of gardens, temples and pavilions in the Chinese style. In the prayer hall hang Chinese lanterns burning fluorescent lamps. The side galleries of the compound contain beautifully carved furniture and

Buried for 2,000 years, a terracotta charioteer still reins in his fallen steeds.

screens. (Xi'an's Muslim minority, including descendants of Silk Road travellers, adds to the flavour of the city—and its shops and restaurants.)

The **Shaanxi Provincial Museum,** occupying a one-time Confucian temple, holds a rich store of art works and rare artefacts—funerary figurines, traditional paintings, ancient household equipment, and huge bronzes masterfully cast 3,000 years ago. But attention here focuses on the museum's famous **Forest of Steles.** This library of inscribed stone slabs, including half a million words of Confucius, carved in the 9th century, documents the history of Chinese culture and calligraphy. You don't

ing country south of the urban area. Grass grows from the pagoda's roofs.

The Big Wild Goose Pagoda was built to house precious Buddhist texts brought back from India by Xi'an's most celebrated pilgrim, an intrepid scholar named Xuanzang. Having survived years of sandstorms and blizzards, demons and dragons, Xuanzang was feted on his return to the capital in A.D. 645. He spent the next 20 years or so translating his stack of holy books from Sanskrit to Chinese.

Though it's shorter, slimmer and slightly newer than the Big Wild Goose Pagoda, the **Small Wild Goose Pagoda** *(Xiao Yan Ta)* has more floors: 13 at the moment. When it was built, at the beginning of the 8th century, it had 15 tiers, but the top came tumbling down in a Ming-era earthquake. Though the pagoda has been structurally repaired and reinforced, it remains topless.

have to know how to read Chinese to appreciate the evolution of the written language over thousands of years. And the art of calligraphy is exalted here as nowhere else.

During the Tang Dynasty, when the **Big Wild Goose Pagoda** *(Da Yan Ta)* was built, it stood well within the walled city. But Xi'an has since contracted, and now the seven-storey brick pagoda rises in the middle of farm-

The Small Wild Goose Pagoda is several kilometres closer to town than its namesake (nobody is certain how either name originated), but still beyond the worst of the uncommonly chaotic traffic of central Xi'an. In spite of the best efforts of numerous traffic patrolmen and volunteer helpers, the buses, trucks, horse carts, tractors, official cars, bicycles, hand carts and pedestrians make their own laws here.

Banpo Village 半坡村

The oldest of the region's archaeological wonders was found about 10 kilometres (6 miles) east of Xi'an. Six thousand years ago a village, evidently thriving, occupied this farmland. Traces of habitation came to light in the 1950s, when workmen were digging the foundations for a new factory. Of course, **Banpo Village** took precedence over a factory, and a museum and viewing hall mark the spot today.

Curiously, you have to climb a flight of stairs to reach the dig, which lies rather higher than the neighbouring terrain. From a series of walkways you look down on the outlines of houses, ovens, storage areas and graves. You can follow the evolution of the dwelling from round or semi-underground to a rectangular house with slanting roofs—the prototype of the typical Chinese house.

On display in the **Banpo Museum,** next to the site, are some of the objects found in the course of excavations: axes and fishhooks, utilitarian pots as well as artistically decorated ceramics. Signs with English explanations analyze the skills of the Banpo villagers, ingenious Stone-Age pioneers.

Qin Army Vaults 秦始皇兵马俑

China's greatest archaeological attraction, the terracotta warriors of the Qin Army, stand in battle formation about 30 kilometres (nearly 20 miles) east of Xi'an. The life-sized (and slightly larger) infantrymen and archers, officers and their horses symbolically guard the tomb of the first Qin emperor.

Well before his death in 210 B.C., Qin Shi Huangdi conscripted hundreds of thousands of his subjects to build a suitably impressive tomb. That tomb, beneath an artificial hill nearby, has yet to be excavated. But the novel conceit of guarding it with thousands of pottery soldiers was revealed by accident in 1974, when local peasants dug a well. The discovery created a world-wide sensation.

An arched structure resembling an aircraft hangar has been built to protect the dig from the weather. Walkways permit tourists a bird's-eye survey of the site, revealing the deployment of the troops and the crumbled state in which most of the figures were found. (The vaults were badly damaged by fire, evidently a few years after they were built.)

The nearby **museum** displays the figures themselves. You'll appreciate the touches that made each of the warriors an individual—a varying headdress, a moustache or beard, or a different look about the eyes. The eager, graceful horses also have distinctive traits. Originally the colours applied to the figures were bright, but they were mostly neutralized by the fire and the passage of centuries.

A large free market operates just outside the fence. Peasant women and children sell homemade toys, brightly coloured knitwear and novelties to the tourist throngs. Haggling is definitely in order.

Hua Qing Hot Springs 华清池

History and natural beauty mingle easily at Hua Qing Hot Springs, a popular digression for tourists on the way to or from the Qin Army excavations. The spa's hot, mineral-rich waters and situation on Black Horse Mountain (*Li Shan*) attracted a series of royal patrons, starting as far back as the 8th century B.C. The emperors and their retinue required suitable accommodation, so the place was provided with delightful pavilions, pools and gardens.

One particular attraction draws crowds of eager Chinese tourists: the large, mosaic bottomed **Oval Tub** used by Lady Yang Gui Fei, favourite concubine of the Tang Emperor Xuan Zong (who reigned from A.D. 712 to 756). Lady Yang was known as a famous beauty, and her portrait, hanging in her former dressing room, attests to the fact. Though she was dear to the emperor, Lady Yang's extravagances and intrigues angered courtiers. The end of the story is so sad it has been the subject of classic poems and plays: when mutinous troops demanded her head, the intimidated emperor acceded, to save his throne. After she was taken away and strangled, the poets report, the emperor wept. Then he abdicated.

A bizarre episode in modern history also took place at Hua Qing Hot Springs in 1936. It was known as the Sian Incident. Chiang Kai-shek, using the spa as a Nationalist base, was betrayed to the Communists by two of his generals. But before he could be abducted, the Generalissimo fled up the mountainside in his slippers. The place where they finally captured him is now enshrined by a **pavilion** called "Chiang Was Caught Here". Thanks to mediation by Zhou Enlai, Chiang was soon released in exchange for an agreement on a united front with the Communists in the war against the Japanese invaders.

Xianyang Museum 咸阳博物馆

The first Qin emperor, who commissioned those life-sized terracotta warriors, made his capital about 20 kilometres (12 miles) north-west of Xi'an at what is now the industrial city of Xianyang. When the dynasty was overthrown in 206 B.C., the capital and its palaces were destroyed, so the area has long intrigued archaeologists—a state of affairs that has greatly enriched the local museum.

Xianyang Museum occupies a restored Confucian temple; the compound itself is an interesting example of 14th-century architecture. But the most stunning exhibit is inside, behind glass: a miniature army of thousands of ceramic soldiers, each about as tall as a year-old baby. A few, mysteriously, look sideways, with one arm raised; it is suspected they were archers. Originally all the troops were armed with the pikes or lances of 2,000-year-old technology. These Han figures were found in a tomb 22 kilometres (14 miles) from Xianyang. Nor does the museum neglect the earlier Qin Dynasty; three halls are devoted to the achievements of that era.

Qian Ling 乾陵

The tombs of notables of the Tang Dynasty, dug into a mountainside (Liang Shan) about 80 kilometres (50 miles) north-west of Xi'an, provide an intriguing look at the level of art and culture reached in China while Europe was immersed in the Dark Ages.

The principal tomb belongs to the third Tang emperor, Gao

A pottery army stands vigilant guard before the tomb of Qin Shi Huangdi. A triumph for archaeology, this recent discovery has thrown new light on the customs, dress and military organization of the Qin Dynasty (221–206 B.C.).

186

Zong, and his ambitious widow, Wu Zetian, who had herself promoted to the rank of empress in A.D. 691—the only woman to hold such power in all Chinese history. Though their tomb has not been excavated, the ostentation of the exterior suggests what may lie within. For instance, there are giant stone **sculptures** of animals and birds and generals and (now headless) ambassadors. The countryside, too, is remarkable—arduously terraced farmland more than a thousand metres (3,300 feet) above sea level. Tombs of princes and imperial officials abound here, often resembling oversized anthills.

And alongside the Royal Way leading to the tomb of honour you can even see a modern troglodyte village, burrowed into the porous terrain; the local farmers live in cave houses complete with electricity and running water. (A 1983 government survey estimated that 40 million people live in caves in the Yellow River basin.)

Satellite tombs in the area have revealed exquisite murals, some of which may be viewed in the original, others in careful reproductions. A famous set of **frescoes** in the tomb of Prince Zhang Huai depicts an animated polo match, a hunting expedition, a reception for foreign diplomats, and—most movingly—a scene in a court cloister with a young concubine looking longingly at a bird in flight.

Another tomb with a steeply inclined entrance, that of the Princess Yong Tai, has a **mural** full of intriguing details showing court maidens attending the princess (who was to die at the age of 17). The satellite tombs also reveal brightly coloured ceramic figurines, stone carvings and memorial tablets.

A souvenir shop adjoins the small museum at the tomb of Princess Yong Tai (also known as Li Xianhui). There are "unofficial" shopping opportunities, too, at many of the archaeological sites. Outside the Qian tomb, for instance, local children hawk homemade souvenirs as well as ancient coins, very likely authentic farmers' finds.

City tours of Xi'an often include other shopping possibilities—for instance, a visit to the local cloisonné factory, described as one of China's major producers of this form of enamelled metalware. Or the jade factory, where artisans take up to six months to create a single figurine from a piece of indestructible stone.

People from all over visit the hot springs of Hua Qing, for centuries a favourite resort of China's emperors.

189

YANGZHOU 扬州
(*Yangchow*)

Like the better known towns farther south in Jiangsu Province —Suzhou and Wuxi— the small city of Yangzhou balances the bustle of the Grand Canal with the tranquillity of gardens and lakes.

Because of its proximity to the Canal and the Yangtze and Huahe rivers, Yangzhou has been an important transportation junction for many centuries. At one time, a thousand years ago, it was the capital of the Southern Wu Kingdom. In the 13th century Marco Polo pronounced it "a place of great consequence", protected by many troops. By special order of the Great Khan, the Venetian traveller found himself acting as governor of Yangzhou for three years.

Yangzhou's favourite son was a Buddhist monk of the Tang Dynasty, Jian Zhen, who sacrificed his health and almost his life to take his doctrine and Chinese art and sciences over the sea to Japan. In A.D. 759 he designed the Toshodai Temple near Nara, Japan's ancient cultural capital. To this day Japanese pilgrims come to Yangzhou in his memory.

Contributions from Japanese Buddhists paid for the construction of the **Jian Zhen Memorial Hall,** a modern rendering of Tang-Dynasty style, located in the complex of the **Fa Jing Temple** in north-west Yangzhou. Buddhist monks still live in the temple, founded 1,500 years ago but reconstructed in recent times. An unusual building here is the **Flat Hills Hall** (*Ping Shan Tang*), an 11th-century structure recently restored.

Yangzhou's leading beauty spot is **Slim West Lake** (*Shou Xi Hu*), so named because it is long and narrow, as well as reminiscent of Hangzhou's famous West Lake. The Qing Emperor Qian Long found the fishing here so good, it's said, that he boosted imperial appropriations for Yangzhou. Little did he imagine that, to ensure the emperor's angling success, local divers secretly threaded fish onto his line. The Fishing Platform (*Diao Yu Tai*), the scene of these gentle deceptions, still stands.

There are three classical Chinese gardens in Yangzhou: **Ge Garden** (*Ge Yuan*), designed by a noted landscape architect of the Qing Dynasty; **He Garden** (*He Yuan*), devised in the 19th century; and **Yechun Garden** (*Ye Chun Yuan*) featuring a charming pavilion with a thatched roof.

Yangzhou's long artistic tradition finds expression today in the field of handicrafts. The local artisans are well known for lacquerware inlaid with mother of pearl, and also embroidery, jade carving, paper-cuts and handsome reproductions of ancient books.

BRIEFINGS

鞍山 **Anshan,** Liaoning Province. Iron and steel producing city of more than one million. Sharing the skyline with blast-furnace chimneys are traditional upswept roofs of pavilions in the city's roomy parks. Tang Gang Zi Hot Springs, formerly a resort for aristocrats, now includes a steelworkers' sanatorium.

安阳 **Anyang,** Henan Province. Capital of the Shang Dynasty 3,000 years ago, Anyang has fascinated archaeologists for the past half-century. Excavations of the ancient city of Yin have revealed priceless bronzes, pottery and "oracle bones" inscribed with the earliest Chinese writing; examples are on view in a museum near the dig. Anyang also boasts a thousand-year-old pagoda.

包头 **Baotou,** Inner Mongolia. Founded in the 5th century, this "steel city on the prairie" has become the biggest industrial centre of Inner Mongolia. Two Tibetan-style pagodas figure prominently on the sparse sight-seeing agenda.

北戴河 **Beidaihe** *(Peitaihe)*, Hebei Province. Summer resort on the Bohai Gulf, developed in the 1890s by foreigners. Still popular with the foreign diplomatic and business community from Beijing, as well as Chinese officials. Parks, beaches and good food are the top attractions.

长春 **Changchun,** Jilin Province. Historically interesting for its role as capital of Manchukuo (Japanese-occupied Manchuria) in the 1930s and '40s. Capital of Jilin Province, China's main producer of ginseng root, sable fur and deer antler.

从化温泉 **Conghua Hot Springs,** Guangdong Province. Local warlords and Kuomintang officials were among the early patrons of this spa, surrounded by hills covered with bamboo, plum, magnolia and cypress trees. Situated 80 kilometres (50 miles) from Guangzhou (Canton), the springs are popular with Chinese and foreign tourists alike. The mineral water, flowing from 11 different springs, is colourless, odourless and tasteless—but good for you.

大连 **Dalian** *(Dairen)*, Liaoning Province. Ice-free port, summer resort and industrial city of one million, also known as Luda. Because of a history of foreign occupation, the city is an eclectic medley of architectural styles—China seasoned with a dash of Japan, a pinch of old Russia, and a forcible hint of Soviet socialist realism. Across the peninsula from the port are green parks, cosy coves and sandy beaches.

福州 **Fuzhou** *(Foochow)*, Fujian Province. Halfway down the coast between Shanghai and Guangzhou, Fuzhou is the sentimental home of millions of overseas Chinese —where the graves of their forefathers are found. It was one of the Treaty Ports open to foreign settlement in the 19th century. The city is still famous for traditional handicrafts, especially "Foochow Body-less Lacquerware" with as many as 80 coats of lacquer. Thousand-year-old temples stand on nearby hillsides.

Hainan Island. This tropical island, nearly four times the size of Corsica, off the southernmost tip of China, provides China with coffee, coconuts, sugar and rubber. It's also destined for promotion as one of those paradise islands Western tourists dream about. The original inhabitants, members of the Li and Miao minorities, live in the rainforests of the interior, preserving a rich folklore; Han Chinese make up most of the coastal population. The island's biggest city, Haikou, on the north shore, has a bustling street life. The perfect, palm-shaded beaches are on the southern shore—big enough, the Chinese reckon, for a hundred thousand sunbathers.

海南岛

Jingdezhen *(Chingtehchen)*, Jiangxi Province. Jingdezhen has been producing famous pottery since the Han Dynasty. White clay from a nearby mountain made possible very thin, durable,

景德镇

Apples of the Baotou region are bound for the big cities of China; local people live in snug houses of earthen brick.

translucent porcelain. (The mountain, Gaoling, gave its name to kaolin—the clay used to make porcelain.) Tourists visit an ancient kiln as well as modern ceramics factories that turn out copies of classic designs.

拉
萨
Lhasa, Tibet. Only tourists in good physical condition should venture to the capital of the Tibet (Xizang) Autonomous Region,

for the altitude of 3,600 metres (nearly 12,000 feet) taxes heart and lungs. (Oxygen is provided in the guesthouse and on the sight-seeing buses.) In any event, visas and accommodation are scarce even for the most determined travellers. Apart from the majestic Himalayan scenery, the number one attraction in Lhasa is the Potala, a fabulous 13-storey building combining the functions

of palace, fortress, monastery and dungeon. Other temples, reopened since Beijing granted the Tibetans greater religious freedom in 1980, are now on the itinerary as well.

南昌 **Nanchang,** Jiangxi Province. Founded in the Han Dynasty, Nanchang is the provincial capital and main industrial centre of subtropical Jiangxi Province. In 1927 it was the scene of the first

Communist-led armed uprising against the Nationalist forces. Relics of Zhou Enlai and other leaders of the Nanchang Uprising have been preserved in the museum devoted to the insurrection.

Ningbo (*Ningpo*), Zhejiang Province. Down the coast from Shanghai, this port town has a long history of overseas connections. First there was trade with Japan. 宁波

Former residence of Tibet's Dalai Lama, the Potala towers above Lhasa. The palace has 1,000 rooms; most of them lie empty.

memorial temple was begun in 478 B.C., the year after the philosopher's death, and improvements and expansions went on for another two thousand years. The compound contains ceremonial gateways, palaces, pavilions and shrines. The tombs of Confucius and most of his descendants are set among ancient pines and cypresses north of the town.

Shanhaiguan *(Shanhaikuan)*, Hebei Province. Its strategic location made this walled town the site of many important battles over thousands of years. But it is best known as the eastern terminus of the Great Wall. Five huge Chinese characters meaning "The First Pass Under Heaven" mark the two-tiered gate-tower as the starting point of the Wall. Just south of Shanhaiguan is the Bohai Gulf port of Qinhuangdao.

山
海
关

Shenyang, Liaoning Province. In 1625 Shenyang (better known abroad as Mukden) became the capital of the Manchus. The Imperial Palace they built was intended to rival the Forbidden City of Beijing; some 70 buildings contain 300 rooms. It now serves as a museum of history and ar-

沈
阳

Then Portuguese settlers arrived. Finally, a British consulate was established after the Opium Wars. Sights include a thousand-year-old wooden temple and a Ming-Dynasty library in a pretty garden.

曲
阜

Qufu *(Chufu)*, Shandong Province. The birthplace of Confucius has been turned into an architectural ensemble on the scale of the Forbidden City in Beijing. The

195

chaeology. In the 1930s the "Mukden Incident"—a bomb explosion on the railway here—precipitated the Japanese occupation of Manchuria.

深
圳
Shenzhen (*Shumchun*), Guangdong Province. Veteran travellers remember Shumchun as an undistinguished border town on the Hong Kong-to-Canton railway line. But it's now the centre of a Special Economic Zone for joint industrial ventures with capitalists from Hong Kong and Macao. And its tourist potential—beaches and hot springs—is rapidly being developed. Day tours from Hong Kong offer Shenzhen as a glimpse of life in China, but its position in an economic buffer zone makes it atypical.

石
家
庄
Shijiazhuang (*Shihchiachuang*), Hebei Province. This railway junction has grown into a provincial capital of 600,000 people. Foreign tourists are taken to a local hospital dedicated to Dr. Norman Bethune, a Canadian surgeon who worked in China during the Sino-Japanese War and whom the Chinese consider a national hero. The doctor's tomb may be found in the Mausoleum of Martyrs.

泰
山
Taishan, Shandong Province. Taishan, one of China's holy mountains, is famous for its legends and scenery, not its altitude. (It's only about 1,500 metres [5,000 feet] high.) The emperors used to be carried up to the peak. It's a possible day trip from Jinan, the provincial capital, but real enthusiasts spend the night in a simple mountain hostel in the hope of watching the sun rise above the clouds. Hikers catch their breath at mountainside temples, towers, pavilions, gateways, caves and waterfalls. In 1983 a cable-car system went into operation.

Wuhu, Anhui Province. The Yangtze River port of Wuhu has been known by its present name since the Han Dynasty. The population of the city including the agricultural outskirts now exceeds 900,000. Mirror Lake, in the centre of town, quietly contrasts with the drama of the great river at the doorstep. Wuhu is well known for its river fish and crabs and for its lively, unspoiled market.
芜
湖

Xiamen (*Amoy*), Fujian Province. With the construction of a new airport to complement its fine natural harbour, this island on the Taiwan Strait has been designated as a Special Economic
厦
门

The Steps of Heaven lead up the sacred mountain of Taishan.

Zone; major tourist development is under way. The island offers sandy beaches, subtropical parks and a singular history. As one of the 19th-century Treaty Ports, it was settled by Europeans, who are responsible for the nostalgia of the architecture. During the 1950s and '60s Taiwanese artillery exchanged bombardments with the local garrison every other day. But all's quiet now.

Xishuang Banna, Yunnan Province. Tourism is new to this Autonomous Prefecture (Capital Jinghong) on the border of Burma and Laos, mostly populated by members of the Dai nationality (closely tied culturally and ethnically to the people of Thailand). In the humid subtropical climate, thousands of species of trees and plants flourish, as do rare animals, birds and insects. (Wild elephants and a curious variety of primitive monkey figure among protected species.) Excursions include visits to Dai stilt villages.

西双版纳

Yan'an (*Yenan*), Shaanxi Province. This small town in the loess hills north of Xi'an is one of Chinese communism's most celebrated historic sites. The 10,000-kilometre (6,000-mile) odyssey of the Long March, in which the Communists escaped Nationalist harassment and regrouped to fight the Japanese, ended in the

延安

vicinity of Yan'an. Revolutionary landmarks, including caves in which Mao Zedong lived, are the tourist attractions here, along with a restored Song-Dynasty pagoda.

Yantai (*Yentai*), Shandong Province. Year-round fishing craft enliven the port of Yantai (once known as Chefoo). Down the coast is a wide band of sandy beach, popular with Chinese holiday-makers. Nearby farming country supports cherry and apple orchards and vineyards which produce well-known wines and brandies. The Municipal Museum, behind a traditional Chinese gateway, displays both archaeological finds and classical art.

烟台

Yixing (*Yihsing*), Jiangsu Province. The province's biggest producer of bamboo and tea, Yixing is better known for its pottery. "Purple Sand" pottery teapots, in original, graceful designs, are highly prized. The region's green hills conceal caves as grand as Shanjuan Cave, which can be viewed from one of the small tourist boats navigating its underground streams.

宜兴

Yueyang (*Yoyang*), Hunan Province. Flamboyant upswept roofs surmount Yueyang Tower, a Tang landmark rebuilt in Song-Dynasty style. The three-storey

岳阳

tower stands guard over Lake Dong Ting, one of China's biggest lakes. In summer huge lotus flowers rise above the surface of the water. Junshan, an island in the lake endowed with many hills (and legends), produces the rare and fragrant "silver needle" tea.

郑
州

Zhengzhou *(Chengchow)*, Henan Province. A busy railway junction on the main lines from Beijing to the south and west, Zhengzhou is now home to over a million people. It was first settled more than 3,000 years ago; traces of the Shang-Dynasty city wall can still be seen beyond the present city limits. Better preserved ancient relics may be viewed in the Henan Provincial Museum.

镇
江

Zhenjiang *(Chenchiang)*, Jiangsu Province. Set at the intersection of the Yangtze River and the Grand Canal, Zhenjiang is an industrial city surrounded by beautiful mountains. The tallest, Jiao Shan, rising from the river itself, has a functioning monastery. Jin Shan is best known for a soaring pagoda and legendary caves. A Song-Dynasty iron pagoda stands on a third hill, Bei Gu Shan.

A monk performs libations in Xiamen, a traditional Buddhist stronghold.

WHAT TO DO

Shopping

Having watched coachloads of foreign tourists clamouring to buy souvenirs at every stop, from the Forbidden City to the oases of Xinjiang, the Chinese authorities have opened shops wherever visitors go.

For ease of shopping make for one of the Friendship Stores, established in all significant tourist locations. They are essentially for foreigners only. The staff speak several languages and usually have all the patience in the world for repetitive queries. Foreign money may be changed on the premises, and some credit cards are accepted.

But more adventurous travellers may stumble across the same items in one of the neighbourhood stores. There the scene is less relaxed and the language problem may daunt you, but at least you'll catch a glimpse of Chinese consumer society.

In many cities, arts and crafts department stores showcase the output of local artisans; antique shops specialize in old pottery, jewellery, carvings and calligraphy, as well as high quality reproductions.

Since the distribution system is unpredictable, old China hands say you shouldn't take a chance: if you find something you like,

buy it, for it may be on sale nowhere else in China.

Prices are as marked; do not haggle.

Shopping Possibilities

Bargains are rare, but there's much to buy in China's stores, shops and markets. Here's an alphabetically organized listing to start you on your rounds.

Antiques. From fossils to an-

cient coins, Chinese customs regulations prohibit the export of
any cultural relics except those
marked with special wax seals.
And only fairly recent objects are
given the seal. Even so, browsing
is fascinating. Remember that
many knowledgeable buyers have
preceded you. The authorities peg
antique prices to international
levels.

Bamboo products. In the south-

ern regions where bamboo grows,
cottage industries turn out bamboo tea boxes, fans, flutes,
chopsticks, walking sticks and
furniture.

Brocades and silks. Since the
Han Dynasty, China has been

*Xianjiang women sell hand-stitched
patchwork and embroidery in the free
market.*

exporting delicate silk fabrics in brilliant colours. Now you can buy inexpensive raw silk by the metre or exquisite brocades, and silk scarves, ties and blouses.

Bronzeware. Modern versions of traditional hotpots are useful; also bronze pitchers, plates and vases, often engraved with intricate dragon or floral designs.

Carpets and rugs. Luxurious and colourful, oriental rugs of wool or silk are a tempting buy. The big stores catering to foreign tourists arrange for shipping.

China (porcelain). Reproductions of classical designs or modern teapots, cups, plates, vases. Shrewd buyers point out that

The bazaar in Urumqi supplies shoppers with all manner of roots and herbs, spices and seasonings.

price tags always indicate the excellence of porcelain (and cloisonné ware, as well): in the line of Chinese text before the actual price, look for the Chinese symbols for 1, 2 or 3 (one, two or three horizontal lines), meaning first, second or third class. If there's no number at all, it means first class.

Chopsticks. Now that you're becoming familiar with Chinese cooking, you may want to collect appropriate utensils. Elaborate chopsticks are sold in their own fitted carrying cases — handy for a picnic, perhaps, or an emergency.

Cloisonné. The Chinese don't claim to have invented this type of enamelware, but they've been doing it very well for the last several hundred years. Cloisonné is applied to plates, vases and other items.

Ethnic novelties. China's minority nationalities produce a goodly share of exotica: ornaments and figurines, ceremonial knives and swords, skullcaps and other headgear, colourful dresses and shirts, and shaggy sheepskin coats.

Fans. One factory in Hangzhou alone manufactures 10 million fans per year, most of them for export. They come in several hundred varieties, but the best known folding fans are made of fragrant sandalwood or black paper.

Figurines. Ceramic polychrome figurines of historic or legendary personages are popular; also little animals, with the panda the most sought after.

Furniture. Boxwood, mahogany or bamboo screens, chairs and chests with elaborately carved designs recreate the atmosphere of old China. Shipping can be arranged.

Furs. Soft, glossy sable or marten coats are often displayed in Friendship Stores. The styling may not be the latest fashion, but the price tag could make all the difference.

Ginseng. The all-purpose Chinese medicinal herb is becoming well known in the West as a tonic. Small doses of ginseng in tea, wine or soup are claimed to be the secret of enduring vitality.

Herbs and spices. Every market has stands selling fragrant spices. Look above all for varieties particular to the region — in Chongqing, for instance, Sichuan dried peppers. A few fen will buy an exotic gift, especially welcome when the herbs or spices are unknown or unavailable at home.

Ivory. Carvings of remarkable intricacy are a Chinese speciality. But only an expert can distinguish between a genuine tusk and substitute material. Note: there are restrictions on the import of ivory from China to the United States.

Jade. One of the hardest of stones, jade has intrigued the Chinese for at least 3,000 years. Even if you don't believe in its mystic powers, jade's aesthetic appeal cannot be denied.

Kites. In windy Beijing and other Chinese cities high-flying kites are a favourite of children and others. The designs are colourful, original and elaborate.

Lacquerware. Numerous layers of lacquer, individually polished, are applied to trays, cups, vases, boxes. Lacquer also makes the ideal finish for tea and coffee services, since the material resists boiling water as well as the chemical properties of tea and coffee.

Luggage. One answer to the problem of excessive souvenir buying may be to buy additional luggage for carrying it home. The Chinese make good, cheap, sturdy suitcases of all sizes. Or you might pick up a local imitation of a Western executive's attaché case.

Musical instruments. European and Chinese musical instruments — violin, guitar, flute or *pipa* (a sort of ukulele) — are well made and usually well priced.

Paintings. Squadrons of artists make copies of traditional drawings and paintings by hand. A single scroll can take ten days to duplicate, brush stroke by brush stroke. Artists also produce original meditations on venerable themes. The scrolls — landscape details to be glimpsed in sections, not all at once — have the advantage of being already rolled-up for packing.

Paper-cuts. The Chinese, who invented paper, are thought to have devised this decorative art nearly two thousand years ago. With amazing skill, the scissors-wielding paper-cutters produce intricate scenes suitable for framing.

Rubbings and reproductions. Stone rubbings of inscriptions from ancient temples, or of classical calligraphy steles, make popular (and portable) souvenirs. Some museums have shops selling reproductions of their most famous archaeological exhibits — for instance, in Lanzhou, the flying horse. Tiny facsimiles of the Xi'an warriors are now available in many parts of the country.

Seals (name chops) are the traditional Chinese substitute for handwritten signatures. You can have one carved just for you, with your name incised — perhaps in ancient Chinese block characters — in soapstone, plastic, jade or ivory.

Souvenirs. In any local department store or street market you're liable to come across some very Chinese inspirations: acupuncture charts and dolls, those ubiquitous thermos flasks, tea mugs with lids, padded jackets, posters and so on.

Tea. A collection of Chinese teas — black, green, semi-fermented and flower-petal — make an inexpensive, useful and long-lasting souvenir. Tea is often

specially packaged in artistically decorated containers.

Toys. Cheap and unusual children's toys, from cuddly animals to mechanical games, are being manufactured in increasing numbers in China.

Woollens. An unexpected bargain is Cashmere sweaters, in all styles and colours. Other woollens, too, represent good quality, economical purchases.

Entertainment

After a gruelling day of sightseeing, you may not be disappointed to find that an evening's entertainment starts and ends early. Nightlife stays on a high cultural plane, far removed from the nightclub scene of Europe or America, combining amusement with edification in a glittering package few Western impresarios could afford to mount.

Chinese Opera

The Chinese hospitably assume that foreigners can't bear more than about ten minutes of Peking Opera or its regional variations. You may, indeed, find the voices shrill and the mannerisms maddening (many characters seem to spend most of the time fussing with their sleeves, which can unroll to the floor). In which case you won't mind if your guide or host rushes you out of the theatre into the early evening traffic.

But if you persevere you may begin to understand what the Chinese see in this age-old art form. If you fail, you've still enjoyed the splendid costumes, the acrobatics that enliven some versions, and the experience of being in a theatre surrounded by local people.

If possible, familiarize yourself with the plot in advance. (Ideologically uplifting operas were the only ones permitted during the Cultural Revolution, but nowadays classical and modern works are presented.) If you have an interpreter at hand, you'll understand why some scenes animate the audience and others don't. The words of the songs are projected onto screens alongside the proscenium arch to clarify the nuances of a tonal language set to music. Apart from the set pieces, most of the music is percussive and serves to indicate the state of the action.

Props are minimal and the action is subtle—an actor closes an invisible door with a mime gesture, and anyone walking with a

Peking Opera combines music, drama and acrobatics. You can tell the heroes from the villains by their elaborate masks.

riding crop must be understood to be mounted. But the heroic characters couldn't possibly be mistaken for the snarling villains.

Puppets and Acrobats

Popular with adults and children alike, the Chinese shadow play, a two-thousand-year-old folkart form, dramatizes familiar legends. The two-dimensional puppets, manipulated behind a white silk screen, can jump and fly, giving the colourful silhouettes an advantage over the actors in Peking Opera. The busy puppeteers give voice to their characters, often in song. Professional and amateur shadow-play troupes also put on shows with marionettes.

So-called acrobatic shows, staged for tourist groups, are more fun than you might expect. The trapeze artists, of course, are first class and so are the contortionists and human pyramid acts. But they also throw in jugglers and magicians and even comics, and you don't have to understand a word to join the laughter.

Typically, folklore performances, amateur or professional, are organized specially for tourists. Shows feature the costumes, songs and dance of the national minority groups—often as foreign to a Chinese audience as they are to visitors from abroad. To the layman, Uygur music may be indistinguishable from a Turkish lament, and a Sani rice-harvesting dance may look the same as a fertility romp in Indonesia or Mexico. But it is at least uplifting and never lasts very long.

Concerts and Ballet

During the Cultural Revolution, Beethoven and Tchaikovsky were banned and many musicians banished to the countryside for "re-education". So if you go to a concert today, you'll sense the very drama of recovery from mad xenophobia. This needn't obscure the fact that some professional musicians haven't yet reached world standards. But the enthusiasm of players and audience is exciting in itself.

Ballet, a vehicle for ideological indoctrination during the 1960s and '70s, is much less restricted today. Folk legends are often a source of inspiration, and classical European works are sometimes performed, with elaborate costumes, sets and lighting effects.

And a Nightcap

With varying degrees of success, the tourist hotels try to meet foreigners' demands for a quiet place to have a drink and a chat. Only the newest hotels built with international cooperation contain bars reminiscent of those in Europe or America. The others are likely to be quaint rather than cosy.

DINING OUT

While Europeans were still dining on porridge and gnawing bones, the art of good cooking was becoming an important part of China's cultural heritage. French *haute cuisine* competes with it for subtlety and sophistication, but the Chinese have been gourmets a couple of thousand years longer. To this day, no other people confect such a vast variety of dishes from so wide a choice of ingredients, presented with such sensitivity and flair.

Almost every country in the world now has its Chinese restaurants. But the authenticity of the food suffers greatly when essential ingredients are hard to come by and the chef compromises with local tastes. *Real* Chinese cuisine can be one of the highlights of your trip, as memorable as Peking Opera or a walk on the Great Wall. (For details of restaurants and eating hours see p. 237.)

For the Chinese, eating means more than assuaging hunger. (A familiar plague in the nation's history, hunger inspired the Chinese to make the most of foods others might have deemed inedible — snakes, certain fish, and the lining gathered from swallows' nests.) Food in China is a pleasure rich in philosophical profundities. Even the dead are offered food and wine to ensure a more

209

Barbecue Kazakh-style: spiced kebabs are grilled over a charcoal flame.

peaceful journey from this life.

The orchestration of a Chinese meal requires a harmonious progression of tastes, textures and colours. The Chinese revel in contrasts: bitter and sweet, crunchy and tender, the yellow of the pineapple and the red of the pepper. It may seem outlandish to the novice, but the Chinese, for their own good reasons, may eat the sweet course in the middle of the meal and the soup towards the end.

In choosing Chinese food, individual tastes tend to be subordinated to the general welfare. All the dishes are shared; thus, the more people in your party the more chance to sample many flavours. Using chopsticks lengthens the reach, so serving dishes don't have to be passed around, though large circular tables sometimes have revolving platters to facilitate the distribution of the food.

Surviving a Banquet

Tourist groups are often tendered banquets or formal dinners, in which protocol problems compound any uncertainty over the food. The Chinese are most understanding about foreigners' gaffes, but here are a few guidelines to help you avoid making a *faux pas:*

Don't be late. Don't touch any of the food or drink until your host gives the sign that the proceedings have begun. Drink the firewater (usually *mao tai*) in your smallest glass *only* when toasting or replying to a toast. Taste a bit of every dish offered, but start sparingly, for as many as 13 courses may be on the menu. Don't take the last morsel from a serving dish; this might imply that not enough food has been provided. Don't ask for rice, which is not served at banquets; it would be tantamount to demanding a sandwich at a formal dinner.

Regional Cuisines

Profound regional variations developed in Chinese cooking because some ingredients were readily available in one area and not another; tastes, like the climate, differed from place to place.

Most Chinese restaurants overseas feature **Cantonese** food because it was people from Guangdong Province who emigrated far and wide, opened restaurants and introduced new tastes. Steaming and stir-frying capture the natural flavour—as well as the colour and vitamins—of Cantonese food. Look for steamed dumplings filled with meat or shrimp, deep-fried spring rolls, and of course sweet-and-sour pork or prawns. Steamed white rice is the usual accompaniment, though you can order fried rice instead.

Wheat, not rice, is the staple in northern China, so **Peking** cuisine involves noodles or steamed loaves of bread or dumplings. Beijing is the place to try Peking Duck, a legendary delicacy. Every day, specialist restaurants in the capital turn out thousands of freshly-roasted, crispy-skinned ducks. In one of the courses, diners wrap small pieces of skin and meat, sprinkled with green onions and anointed with a sweet bean sauce, in the thinnest of pancakes.

Time and great care go into the cooking and preparation of **Shanghai** cuisine. The flavours are full of happy surprises—sweet or salt accents, plus hints of garlic or vinegar. Meats are often marinated, then braised at length in soy sauce, wine and sugar. But Shanghai is best known for its seafood—steamed freshwater

Applied Chopstickery

After a little practice almost any-one can master chopsticks. First settle the bottom stick firmly at the conjunction of thumb and forefinger, balancing it against the first joint of the ring finger. The second stick pivots around the fulcrum made by the top of the thumb and the inside of the fore-finger. If the sticks were parallel they would be wide enough to pick up an ice-cube. More often they meet at an acute angle. In some regions you are expected to bring the bowl right up to your mouth.

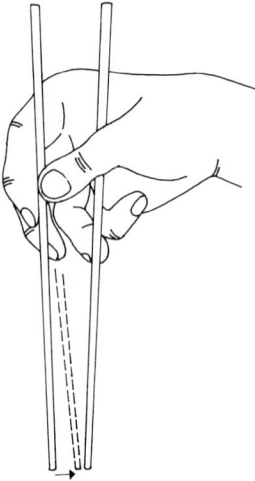

crab, honey-fried eel, braised yellowfish or sautéed shrimp. Nearby Hangzhou has a subtle novelty, shrimp in tea sauce, re-dolent of the unobtrusive flavour of locally grown tea.

Sichuan Province is the source of peppery **Szechuan** recipes, which are much more compli-cated than the first fiery taste would indicate. They combine many elements in unlikely coexis-

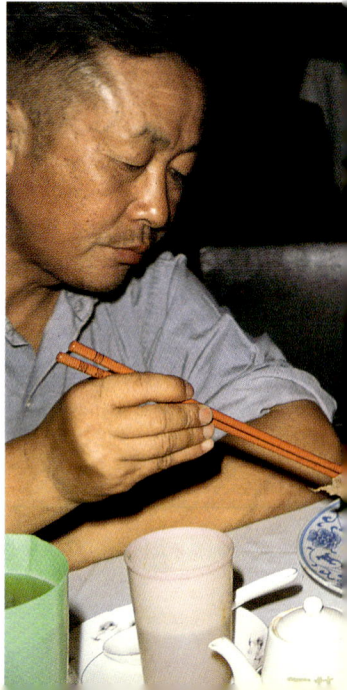

tence—bitter, sweet, fruity, tart, sour. Even beancurd, which many tourists consider hopelessly bland, takes on real character in the hands of cooks in Chengdu or Chongqing. But not everything on the menu is hot; for a bit of relief, try sautéed shredded pork with spring onions and soybeans.

Neighbouring **Hunan** Province also revels in the invigorating possibilities of the chilli pepper. But dishes here turn out less spicy and oily than in their Szechuan counterparts. Gourmets rave about Hunan's chilli-smoked pork or chicken.

Wherever you travel in China look for the local specialities. They may be less celebrated and

Restaurants may be simple, but the food's out of this world.

sophisticated than Shanghai "mock goose" or the sculpted vegetables of a Beijing banquet, but they give you the feeling of the countryside: roast lamb and pilaf rice in far-west Xinjiang; great hunks of mutton in Inner Mongolia; Yunnan's delicately smoked ham served in the thinnest slices; sweet-and-sour fish along the Yangtze. In the northeast, Jilin Province is famous for stewed chicken with ginseng. Neighbouring Heilongjiang Province offers stewed moose nose and braised bear paw with pine nuts. The cooks of Guilin proudly prepare steamed bamboo rat, masked civet, and—great winter

Chinese chefs are past masters of the culinary arts. Peking duck is always roasted to crisp perfection.

tonic, they say—snake broth. "Ground goat" is a euphemism for dog meat, a long-time favourite of Chinese gourmets.

What to Drink

The Chinese have been enjoying wine for thousands of years. Each province or region has its own wine or liqueur, usually rather sweet. It's made from local fruits, flowers or herbs.

Connoisseurs mention red and white wines from Shanghai, the dry white wine of Yantai, and Chefoo white wine. Rice wines come in many varieties, the most venerable is distilled at Shaoxing in Zhejiang Province. In Xi'an you will be offered Xifeng wine, a breathtaking, colourless drink which originated in the Tang Dynasty.

Like the wines, Chinese brandies display regional variations, incorporating ingredients as ingenious as bamboo leaves, chrysanthemums and cloves. The best known *eau de vie*, the staple for banquet toasts, is *mao tai*, fragrant, mellow—but potent.

Beer drinkers use their frothy superlatives in recommending Tsingtao, the hearty, German-style beer brewed from the spring water of Laoshan mountain. A number of local brands are also available in various regions, but none has a comparable international reputation. Mineral waters are also available, as are fruit

juices and soft drinks based on fruit flavours.

Tea is usually offered to guests *before* a banquet, in an anteroom. Teahouses, nowadays something of a rarity in China, are rich in local colour; musicians or story-tellers are on hand to entertain customers who play cards or dominoes by the hour. Chinese tea is taken without sugar or milk. Among the varieties available are black (fermented) tea, fragrant green tea, tea scented with jasmine or magnolia or blends of flowers, and slightly fermented oolong tea.

Breakfast Conventions

In almost any hotel in China, Western tourists are automatically served a European/American-style breakfast, whether they want it or not. This may consist of eggs, toast, butter, jam, and an interpretation of coffee. If you want to try a Chinese breakfast —porridge and buns and perhaps noodles and cold appetizers— you will have to convince the waiter that you really mean it.

In provincial or non-touristic restaurants—and occasionally in the better hotels, as well—you'll notice the Chinese habit of wiping chopsticks and bowls with a paper napkin before a meal. No one takes offence at this precaution.

Note that tipping is just not done in China; you would only fluster the waiter.

BERLITZ-INFO

CONTENTS

A ACCOMMODATION

Accommodation for package tourists is organized in advance in conjunction with the China International Travel Service (CITS), but the name of the hotel is usually only revealed at the last moment by local tour guides. At present only a few Chinese hotels accept individual reservations; the system is being expanded as computers come into wider use. With few exceptions, individual travellers may not request a particular hotel in Beijing, where the local branch of CITS makes assignments based on its own considerations of supply and demand. But in provincial cities there is generally greater flexibility.

Hotels in China range from first class to grimly spartan. The newest hotels, often built with foreign cooperation and expertise, bear the closest resemblance to their counterparts in Europe or America. More adventurous travellers may prefer the charm of old-fashioned establishments in interesting or scenic locations.

In general, hotels in small or remote towns offer few comforts. Air conditioning is relatively unknown in China, but radios and telephones are usually provided, and ever more hotel rooms are now equipped with small refrigerators and television sets.

In almost every room you'll find cups and a large thermos of hot water for making tea. A small container of tea is often supplied, as well. The separate carafe of "drinking water" may not always be trusted; *never* drink water from the tap.

In the larger hotels, there is a service desk on each floor, manned by staff who often speak a bit of English. They keep room keys, handle the laundry, deal with telephone problems and sell cigarettes, snacks, drinks and postcards. Postal, telegraph and telephone desks, a foreign-exchange facility and gift shops are usually located on the ground floor.

A suggestion: when you wander out on your own, even on a brief stroll, take with you a piece of paper with your destination and the hotel's name written in Chinese. This is useful should you have to ask the way or need to direct a taxi.

Could you give me a...?	qǐng nǐ gěi wǒ yì-jiān... haǒ ma	请你给我 ... 好吗?
single/double room	dān-rén-fáng/shuāng-rén-fáng mā	一间单人房／双人房
Does the room come with a private bath?	dài wei-shēng-jiān ma	带卫生间吗?
May I see the room?	wǒ kě-yǐ kàn-kan fáng-jiān mā	我能看一下房间吗?

AIRPORTS *(fēi jī chǎng)*

Six international airports—Beijing (Peking), Shanghai, Guangzhou (Canton), Tianjin, Urumqi and Hangzhou—can accommodate wide-bodied jet airliners. Beijing's Capital Airport is by far the busiest. There are restaurants, snack bars, souvenir stands and a post office. A bank inside the customs zone changes foreign currency, while a duty-free shop operates in the departure lounge.

The municipality of Beijing runs airport buses to the city centre. Taxis are also available for the 40-minute journey into town; drivers mill about outside the customs area. If you are being met by CITS or another organization, you will find a representative waiting for you in customs or, more likely, just outside the door in the terminal.

There is a hotel near Beijing airport, primarily for transit passengers.

Note that small provincial airports may have no taxis on call. Travellers without prior arrangements would be wise to telex ahead to the local tourist office to request transport.

Arrival. Passengers arriving from abroad hand over health certificates (distributed on the plane) to a health officer, and passports, visas and landing cards to immigrations officers, who stamp and return the documents. Completed customs forms are presented to officials in the baggage-claim area; you must retain the carbon copy until you leave the country.

Departure. Be sure to reconfirm your reservation and arrive at the airport before check-in time. Note that you'll be required to pay an airport departure tax in Chinese currency.

C CAR HIRE

Self-drive cars cannot be rented in China, in view of the complexity of city traffic, the state of country roads and the difficulty most foreigners face in deciphering the road signs. But chauffeur-driven cars are readily available. Chinese-made "Shanghai" sedans are the most common; more comfortable Japanese cars are being imported in quantity for tourist use. If you don't want to hire a car for the whole day, it's often possible to arrange for a taxi by the hour plus mileage.

I'd like to hire a car with guide and driver.	wǒ xiǎng zū yí-liàng yǒu xiǎng-dǎo hé sī-jī de qì-chē	我想租一辆有向导和司机的汽车。

CHILDREN

Although relatively few tourists bring their children to China, no special problems should be encountered. But be sure to carry any necessary remedies for coughs, colds and grazes; the Chinese have nothing like the pharmacy you are accustomed to.

What with all the parks and zoos, some amusing outings can be arranged. And the acrobats, jugglers and puppet shows are guaranteed to delight any child. Baby-sitters, however, are virtually unheard of in China. Hotel staff can usually work out something informally.

CIGARETTES, CIGARS, TOBACCO

Shops sell a wide variety of Chinese cigarettes. American brands, manufactured under licence in China, are also available, as well as Bulgarian and North Korean competitors. Chinese connoisseurs relish Sichuan cigars—leaf tobacco wrapped in paper. Pipe-smokers may have to make do with leaf tobacco.

Smoking is barred in theatres, cinemas and on buses.

Give me ... please.	qǐng gěi wǒ...	请给我……
a packet of cigarettes	yī-hé yān	……一盒烟
a box of cigars	yī-hé xuě-jiā-yān	……一盒雪茄烟
some matches	huǒ-chái	……火柴

CLIMATE AND CLOTHING

China is a vast country encompassing a variety of different climates. Summer lasts more than six months of the year in Guangzhou

(Canton) but flits past in only 15 days in far western Urumqi. In January the mean temperature in Harbin, in the north-east, is a deep-frozen –19.7° C (–3° F) while Nanning in the south basks in 12.9° C (55° F). The chart below should help you plan your wardrobe.

In general, the best seasons all over China are spring and autumn, when medium-weight clothing is appropriate in most areas. Be sure to pack sweaters and rainwear. For winter, a warm overcoat is essential. Woollen underwear is a boon; gloves, mufflers and hats make worthy accessories. All can be bought on the spot, if necessary, at reasonable prices. The Chinese tend to dress in several layers of clothing, facilitating quick reactions to changes of temperature.

Tourists dress with relative informality, though business visitors usually wear suits and ties for important meetings or banquets. By all means avoid ostentation.

Some average monthly temperatures:

		J	F	M	A	M	J	J	A	S	O	N	D
Beijing	°F	25	28	39	55	68	77	79	77	68	55	39	27
	°C	–4	–2	4	13	20	25	26	25	20	13	4	–3
Guangzhou	°F	57	59	64	72	79	81	84	84	81	75	68	59
	°C	14	15	18	22	26	27	29	29	27	24	20	15
Shanghai	°F	37	39	46	57	66	75	82	82	75	64	55	43
	°C	3	4	8	14	19	24	28	28	24	18	13	6
Xi'an	°F	27	36	46	57	68	79	81	79	68	55	45	34
	°C	–3	2	8	14	20	26	27	26	20	13	7	1
Guilin	°F	46	48	56	65	74	79	83	82	78	69	59	50
	°C	8	9	13	18	24	26	29	28	26	21	15	10

COMMUNICATIONS

Post offices *(yóu-jú)*. Hotels have branch post offices or postal service desks, open seven days a week (see HOURS), selling stamps, writing paper and postcards. Chinese envelopes are generally made without glue, and so are some stamps—which explains the presence of a gluepot on the counter.

Airmail letters and postcards take up to ten days to reach overseas destinations; surface mail travels extremely slowly.

The Chinese post office has no facilities for poste-restante (general delivery) mail. Since confirmed hotel reservations are rare, this poses a problem. If you expect to receive mail while in China, ask correspondents to address letters c/o CITS in various cities on your itinerary; they should also write on the envelope your tour number, if you're on a package tour, as well as the tour operator's name.

Telephone *(diàn-huà)*. You can make local calls from your hotel room or from any public telephone—usually without charge. Coin-operated street telephones, which are rare, cost 4 fen (two 2-fen coins). Long-distance and international calls must be connected by the operator. Fill out an order form at the service desk on your floor and take the call in your room, or at the desk itself. Rates vary, depending on whether the call is "regular" or "urgent". Reverse-charge (collect) calls may be made.

Telegraph *(diàn-bào)* and **telex** *(yòng-hù diàn-bào)*. The tariffs for international telegrams vary according to the destination and priority (normal or express). Domestic telegrams and overseas radiograms may be dispatched from the postal desks of most hotels.

Telex service cannot always be obtained. In most hotels the client is expected to punch the telex tape, stand by for the connection (meaning unpredictable delays) and actually transmit the message. The charge depends on the time the overseas circuit is in use. Facsimile service, most useful for transmitting documents in Chinese, is available in some cities.

I would like some stamps, please.	qǐng gěi-wǒ jǐ-zhāng yóu-piào	请给我几张邮票。
Where's a mailbox?	xìn-xiāng zài-nǎr	信箱在哪里?
Where's the telephone?	diàn-huà zài nǎr	电话在哪里?
I would like to send a telegram.	wǒ xiǎng dǎ diàn bào	我想打电报。

COMPLAINTS

China's tourist industry is in its infancy, and formal procedures for complaints have yet to be developed. The whole issue is complicated by the oriental problem of "saving face": public criticism of any individual is deemed unjustifiably cruel. A quiet word with your guide will be far more effective than an open demonstration of dissatisfaction. And losing your temper is the worst possible reaction.

CONVERSION CHARTS

China uses the metric system, but traditional measurements endure in the marketplace. First, the standard conversions:

Temperature

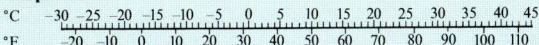

Length

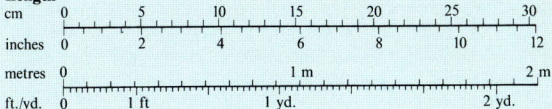

Weight

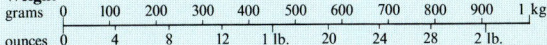

Fluid measures

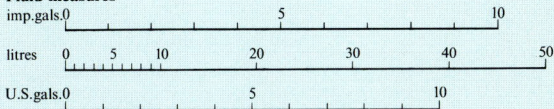

Kilometres to miles

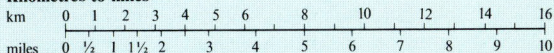

The Chinese market system

Length:

1 *shichi* = 0.33 metre = 1.09 foot	1 *shili* = 0.5 kilometre = 0.31 mile
1 metre = 3 *shichi* = 3.28 feet	1 kilometre = 2 *shili* = 0.62 mile

Area:

1 *mu* = 0.07 hectare = 0.16 acre   1 hectare = 15 *mu* = 2.47 acres

Fluid measure:

1 *sheng* = 1 litre = 0.22 gallon

Weight:

1 *jin* = 0.5 kilogram = 1.10 pound
1 kilogram = 2 *jin* = 2.2 pounds

COURTESIES

A smile is your best good-will gesture in China. Be yourself, of course, but keep in mind some Chinese sensibilities.

Physical contact usually offends the Chinese. Don't put your arm around a Chinese, for instance, in posing for a picture; a jolly slap on the back would be in very bad taste. Avoid public displays of affection, which scandalize older Chinese. Modesty in dress is also recommended.

Don't be afraid to discuss politics, religion or social problems, but refrain from polemics or disrespect to the country, its system or leaders.

Tour groups are sometimes welcomed to a city or an event by applause. The proper response is to applaud in return.

Try to maintain an oriental degree of patience, even if everything goes wrong. Don't blame your guide; it probably isn't his fault. And never let your temper show, for this would be losing face.

At banquets you *must* raise a glass and drink something — a sip of lemonade, juice, anything — when a toast is proposed, no matter how often this occurs. And don't be late for a party or business appointment; punctuality is important to the Chinese.

CRIME AND THEFT

Crime, of course, exists in China as in all countries, but official statistics show the incidence is very low in comparison with Western societies. Cases of crime against foreign visitors are rare, though it is always wise to be wary of pickpockets and petty thieves. However, there are frequent reports of tourists who have misplaced valuables and had them returned. And you can walk freely at any time of day or night without fear.

Ironically, foreign tourists themselves sometimes turn to "crime". Souvenir hunters tempted to appropriate ashtrays or chopsticks should consider the moral issue and the consequences: a waiter or hotel employee will be charged the price of replacing the stolen item.

CUSTOMS, ENTRY AND EXIT REGULATIONS

Travel to China is new, and procedures can be complicated. First there were business visits by invitation only, then tours by groups on rigid programmes, then more flexible package tours, and finally independent individual travel. The regulations change more quickly than books can be updated. For the latest information, be sure to consult a qualified travel agent.

A great deal of advance planning and paperwork go into the preparation for a trip to China. Filling out all the forms will tax your patience and good humour: for example, on the visa application, they ask you to list — in triplicate — all the jobs you've ever had, plus your religion and political party. But officials are unfailingly courteous, and the only suspense you're likely to experience will be the wait for an inscrutable customs officer to decipher your handwriting.

224

Visas. Every visitor to China must possess a valid passport and a visa issued in advance by the Chinese authorities. Tour groups may be issued group visas—a single document listing the names and particulars of all the participants. The paperwork in this case is handled by the travel agency, and the visa charge is usually included in the overall cost of the trip.

Independent travellers, whether tourists or businessmen or professional visitors, must apply for visas at Chinese consulates, or at offices of the China International Travel Service (CITS) and the China Travel Service (CTS). In practice, travel agencies responsible for the general arrangements normally expedite the issuing of the documents. Additional charges are levied for individual visas, as well as for urgent service, if required. The minimum time for delivery varies from one day (Hong Kong) to three or four days in most other places.

Health requirements. No special inoculation certificates are required, except for passengers arriving in China within six days of leaving or transiting an area infected by yellow fever. Precautions against malaria are recommended for travellers planning to visit certain low-lying rural areas. It's wise to consult your doctor before departure.

Customs regulations. Before arrival you will have filled out a baggage-declaration form listing any watches, jewellery, cameras or electronic gadgets in your possession. When you leave China at the end of your tour, you may be asked to prove that you are taking with you all the items on the list, except for goods declared as gifts.

In general, it is forbidden to carry into China the following: arms and explosives, radio transmitting equipment, Chinese currency, material deemed morally or ideologically subversive, and habit-forming drugs.

The duty-free allowance for tourists entering China consists of two bottles of alcoholic beverages (not exceeding ¾ litre), 400 cigarettes, food, clothing and medicine for personal use, and any quantity of foreign currency.

Leaving China. You must present the carbon copy of your baggage-declaration form to customs officials on departure. The officer on duty may ask you to produce any or all items listed (cameras, watches, etc.). Keep receipts of purchases made in China in case any questions arise; note that antiques may not be exported from China unless a special wax seal is attached. Chinese Foreign Exchange Certificates may be exported; normal Chinese currency (RMB) may not. To change money on departure you must show your exchange receipts.

| *I have nothing to declare.* | wǒ méi-yǒu yào-shēn bào de dōng-xī | 我没有要申报的东西。 |

E ELECTRIC CURRENT

In principle the voltage everywhere in China is 220 volts, 50 cycles. In practice the voltage lapses significantly from time to time. Socket types and sizes vary, but adaptors can often be borrowed from the hotel.

EMBASSIES AND CONSULATES *(dà-shǐ-guǎn; lǐng-shì-guǎn)*

Australia	15 Dongzhimen Wai St., Beijing, tel. 522331
Canada	10 Sanlitun Rd., Beijing, tel. 521475
Great Britain	11 Guanghua Rd., Beijing, tel. 521961
New Zealand	1 Dong'er St., Ritan Rd., Beijing, tel. 522731
U.S.A.	2 Xiushui Dong St., Jianguomenwai, Beijing, tel. 522033

EMERGENCIES

See also EMBASSIES AND CONSULATES, HEALTH AND MEDICAL CARE, POLICE, etc.

Police emergency: dial 110.

Call the police!	jiào jǐng chá	叫警察
Careful!	xiǎo-xīn	小心
Danger!	wēi-xiǎn	危险
Fire!	huǒ	火
Get a doctor!	qǐng yī-shēng	请医生
Help!	jiù-rén a	救人啊!
I'm ill.	wǒ bìng le	我病了
I'm lost.	wǒ mí-lù le	我迷路了

G GETTING TO CHINA

Package tours to China often include stops in Hong Kong or Tokyo. Here you can recover from jet lag and take advantage of the chance to shop and enjoy the bright lights. Hong Kong is the easiest place to organize last-minute visas and travel arrangements. There are air, rail, road and sea links between Hong Kong and nearby Guangdong Province, as well as more distant destinations in China. Many travel agencies in Hong Kong offer a variety of all-inclusive China tours, from a one-day excursion across the border to a full two- or three-week agenda taking in major cities and sights. Independent travellers can make arrangements in Hong Kong through the local offices of China Travel Service (CTS) or China International Travel Service (CITS). (CTS handles travel for Overseas Chinese, while CITS, or Luxingshe, is responsible for foreign tourists.)

From North America

Direct flights to China operate from the West Coast. Some airlines link North America to Beijing via Tokyo or Hong Kong. It is also possible to travel by way of Europe. (In certain cases this may save money, to compensate for the time lost.) If time and money are of secondary importance, look into round-the-world fares; some airlines or groups of airlines offer special tariffs and unlimited stopovers as incentives.

From Europe

The Chinese airline, CAAC (Civil Aviation Administration of China), and cooperating European airlines offer flights to Beijing (and sometimes Shanghai) from London, Frankfurt, Paris and Zurich. The airlines of certain countries en route, such as India, Pakistan, Iran or the U.S.S.R., advertise bargain fares.

From Australia and New Zealand

There are several regular scheduled flights from Melbourne, Sydney and Auckland to Beijing or Shanghai. All require stopovers in either Hong Kong, Tokyo or Manila, sometimes with an overnight stay.

GUIDES AND INTERPRETERS *(xiǎng-daǒ; fān-yì)*

Package-tour clients are sometimes overwhelmed with guides—an escort from the travel agency, a Chinese "national" guide, a coordinator attached to one of the major offices of CITS, and a "local" guide who knows the sights of a particular city or region. Independent tourists are not obliged to use the services of a guide/interpreter, though, in general, a guide permits you to use your time more efficiently, eliminating the problems of reservations and transport and providing immediate answers to most of your questions.

The qualifications of CITS guides vary considerably. During the recent expansion of tourism, many linguists or almost-linguists were drafted as guides—whether they wanted the jobs or not. But a knowledgeable guide will greatly enhance your enjoyment and understanding of China.

H HAIRDRESSERS AND BARBERS (lǐ fà diàn)

The larger hotels usually have a hairdresser and a barber shop. The service is good and extemely cheap by Western standards. The treatment may include a head and neck massage, which is most relaxing. Tipping is not permitted.

I would like a haircut, please.	qǐng gěi wǒ lǐ-fà	我想理发。
Don't cut it too short.	bú-yào jiǎn-de tài-duǎn	请别理得太短。
I'd like it cut and shaped.	wǒ yào lǐ fà hé zuòfā	我要理发和做发。
shampoo and set	xǐ-tou he zuò tóufa	洗头和做发。
permanent wave	diàn-tāng	电烫
tint	rǎn-fà	染发

HEALTH AND MEDICAL CARE

No special health difficulties face the visitor to China, but you should consult your doctor before your trip, to anticipate potential problems. Take with you any essential medications, as it is difficult or impossible to find many items in a Chinese pharmacy. If you plan to visit one of the regions in which malaria occurs, you must begin treatment *before* your trip, and continue for a specified time after leaving the affected area.

The minor ailments that most often seem to strike foreign tourists are coughs, colds and sore throats. Digestive upsets occasionally result from too much banqueting, though the food itself is normally prepared under demanding hygienic conditions.

Should you require medical care in China, your guide or hotel desk clerk or the local CITS office will call a doctor, or arrange for you to be taken to a hospital. Considering the language problem, it's a relief to have an interpreter on hand when discussing symptoms and treatment: there is no reason to expect that your doctor, however qualified in medicine, understands one word of English.

Foreign tourists treated in a Chinese hospital must pay a registration fee plus the cost of any medicine prescribed. There is a separate, additional charge in case of hospitalization.

Treatment may involve a combination of modern and traditional medicine—perhaps some tablets to swallow and some herbs to infuse. Acupuncture has wide applications in Chinese medicine, and foreign tourists suffering from colds have been offered an almost painless cure-by-needles. All Chinese doctors are trained in acupuncture as well as in Western medicine.

I need a doctor—quickly.	wǒ yào mǎ shang zhǎo yī shēng	我要马上找医生。
I've got a pain here.	wǒ zhè-li tòng	我这里痛。
headache	tóu tòng	头痛
sore throat	hóu-lóng tòng	喉咙痛
stomach ache	wèi tòng	胃痛

HOURS

Shops. Friendship Stores and department stores are usually open from 9 a.m. to 7 p.m. (8 p.m. in summer), seven days a week. Local shops sometimes stay open later.

Banks in hotels open from 7.30 or 8 a.m. to around 7 p.m., with a break for lunch. (Generally, the larger the hotel, the later the foreign exchange facility stays open.) Money may also be changed on Sunday mornings.

Post office branches in hotels operate from 8 a.m. to 6 p.m., Monday to Saturday, and Sunday mornings from 8 a.m. to noon.

Hairdressers stay open until at least 7 p.m., usually later in hotels.

Museum hours are from 9 a.m. to 4 p.m., six days a week; the usual closing day is Monday.

LANGUAGE

L

Chinese is the native tongue of more people than any other of the world's languages. Yet communication between Chinese can be difficult. The written language that binds them is universal, but spoken Chinese is fragmented into dialects, some of them mutually incomprehensible. In the interests of national unity and understanding, the government vigorously encourages the use of *putonghua*, a national language (known abroad as Mandarin Chinese) based on the dialect spoken in Beijing. But regional traditions are hard to demolish, even for a worthwhile cause.

Chinese is a tonal language; each syllable has a different meaning depending on the pitch or musical inflection it receives. If you speak in a monotone, you will not be understood.

Written Chinese—the pictographs that have told the story of China for thousands of years—has no relation to the sound of the spoken language. In the interests of greater literacy, the Communists have simplified many of the traditional characters, but not enough to make it easy for foreigners. They have also inaugurated a universal system for romanizing Chinese words: Pinyin, meaning phonetic transcription, is the reason Peking is now written Beijing.

Pronouncing Pinyin has its own nuances and complications. Among the biggest stumbling blocks are the following consonants —accompanied by approximate pronunciations.

c	like **ts** in the word i**ts**
g	always as in **g**ive
h	like **ch** in Scottish lo**ch**
j	like **j** in **j**eer
q	similar to **ch** in **ch**eer
x	aspirated **s**
z	like **ds** in ki**ds**
zh	like **j** in **j**ug

English is the most widely spoken foreign language in China. Millions of Chinese have been studying basic English in school and through television. The great majority, unfortunately, know only a few standard phrases, and conversations can become painfully stilted. Hotel and airline employees and others who deal with foreigners have usually learned enough English to cope with everyday problems. Tour guides are trained to specialize in one or more foreign languages, but not all of them have a firm grasp of English. To make yourself understood, you may have to speak very slowly, clearly and simply.

The Berlitz phrase book CHINESE FOR TRAVELLERS covers most of the situations you are likely to encounter in China.

Do you speak English?	nǐ huì shuō yīng yǔ ma	你会说英语吗?
Do you speak German/French?	nǐ huì shuō dé yǔ/fǎ yǔ ma	你会说德语/法语吗?
I don't understand.	wǒ bū míng bǎi	我不明白。

LAUNDRY AND DRY-CLEANING *(shī xǐ; gān xǐ)*

Hotels process laundry and dry-cleaning quickly and efficiently. Most hotels provide their guests with laundry bags; if you're in a hurry, deliver the filled bag to the service desk on your floor; otherwise it will be picked up when the room is cleaned. Laundry is usually returned within 24 hours, but dry-cleaning may take an extra day in all but the biggest hotels.

I would like these clothes...	qǐng gěi wǒ bǎ zhè-xiē yi-fú...	我要这些衣服
cleaned	gān xǐ	干洗
ironed	tàng	烫
washed	xǐ	洗
I would like it as soon as possible.	wǒ jín xū zheìge	我急需这个。

LOST PROPERTY

In China the property of foreigners is so conspicuous that it doesn't usually stay lost for long. Thus the Beijing Public Security Bureau has returned to foreign visitors and residents their cars, motorbikes, bicycles, cameras, radios, television sets and even considerable quantities of cash. If you lose something, start the search by informing your CITS guide or the hotel desk.

I've lost my wallet/ my handbag/ my passport.	wǒ diǒu le qiánbao/ shoǔtí bāo/ hùzhào	我丢了钱包/手提包/护照。

MAPS

M

Local tourist authorities often issue free sketch maps of a city's sightseeing spots and principal avenues, available at hotels and the tourist office. More detailed maps of all the main tourist cities, prepared by the Cartographic Publishing House of Beijing, are sold at bookstores and hotel newsstands. The maps in this book were prepared by Falk-Verlag, Hamburg, which also publishes a map of China with street plans of Beijing, Shanghai and Guangzhou.

MEETING PEOPLE

The Chinese are often keen to practise their English, though conversational possibilities are restricted. But sign language goes a long way, and a friendly approach normally elicits a like response. You can enter any public place or street, but some tourists carry the meet-the-people campaign too far; don't barge into a house or apartment without a specific invitation. In some restaurants, foreigners are assigned to special rooms. Don't insist on being seated with the Chinese diners, as it would only cause embarrassment to the staff and customers alike.

MONEY MATTERS

Currency. China's two-tier currency system is almost bound to confuse you. The standard currency, called *renminbi* or people's money (RMB) is based on the *yuan*, divided into 100 *fen*. Ten fen makes a *jiao*. However, foreign exchange bureaus also dispense a second currency called Foreign Exchange Certificates (FEC) in denominations of 1 and 5 jiao (= 10 and 50 fen) and 1, 5, 10, 50 and 100 yuan. Friendship Stores and other establishments catering primarily to foreigners accept only FEC, not RMB. In some small towns, merchants may not accept FEC, simply because they have never heard of them. FEC may be taken out of China, but RMB may not (see also under CUSTOMS, ENTRY AND EXIT REGULATIONS).

Banks and currency exchange (see also HOURS). Foreign currency and traveller's cheques may be exchanged for FEC in hotels and Friendship Stores. You'll have to show your passport. Keep your receipt, in case you want to convert excess Chinese money to foreign currency when leaving the country.

Credit cards and traveller's cheques. Credit cards are accepted more and more in tourist areas; look for the familiar emblems in hotels, restaurants and Friendship Stores. In some major cities personal cheques are accepted on presentation of certain credit cards, though it may entail a trip to the bank. Traveller's cheques are recognized at the money-exchange counters of hotels and shops almost everywhere in China.

I would like to change some dollars/ pounds.	wǒ xiǎng duì-huàn yī xiē měi-yuán/ yīng-bàng	我要兑换一些美元/英镑
Where can I cash a traveller's cheque?	nǎr kě-yǐ duì-huàn lǚ-xíng zhī-piào	我在哪里能兑换旅行支票?
I have a credit card.	wǒ yǒu yì-zhāng xìn-yòng-kǎ	我有信用卡。

NAMES

According to Chinese practice, the surname or family name—usually only one syllable—comes first. You would use the prefix Mr., Miss or Mrs. with the surname; the given or first name alone is only used among intimate friends or family.

Businessmen travelling to China are advised to carry visiting cards, preferably with a Chinese translation on the reverse side. The Chinese are inveterate exchangers of business cards.

NEWSPAPERS AND MAGAZINES

Some leading foreign newspapers and magazines are sold at the news kiosks of major hotels in Beijing, Shanghai and Guangzhou. The *International Herald Tribune* and the *Asian Wall Street Journal*, both printed in Hong Kong, arrive with about one day's delay.

The Chinese English-language newspaper, *China Daily*, can be found at hotels and newsstands in most cities, though with considerable delays in the hinterland. It covers Chinese and foreign news plus tourist features, sports, even stock-market reports. Official periodicals like *Beijing Review* and *China Pictorial* are widely available in many languages.

Where can I buy an English-language publication?	wǒ zài nǎli néng mǎi-dào yīng-wén shū jí	我在哪里能买到英文书籍?

PACKING

Informal attire is the rule. Comfortable walking shoes are essential. If you find you lack some item of clothing, a serviceable substitute can probably be bought locally.

On the other hand, many of the small oddments that we take for granted are rarely available in China. The Friendship Stores, which cater to foreigners, attempt to fill the gap, but with limited success. Even if the main Friendship Store in Beijing stocks disposable razors and paper handkerchiefs, the tourist who needs them in the provinces is probably out of luck.

Here is a list of some of the things you are *not* likely to find on sale in Chinese shops: Patent medicines (including aspirin, cold medicine and stomach remedies, ointments and adhesive plasters), tampons, Western cosmetics, shampoo, insect repellent, sun-tan lotion, cough drops, batteries, some sizes of films, certain brands of cigarettes, instant coffee, cold-water laundry powder.

PHOTOGRAPHY

Friendship Stores sell some international brands of film but not necessarily the size or type you need. To be sure you don't run out, pack an adequate supply—keeping in mind that you'll probably use more film than usual, in view of all those fabulous photo possibilities. Relatively quick film processing is available in main cities, but for reliability most tourists prefer to develop film at home.

As a courtesy, always ask permission before taking a close-up of a Chinese. Don't force anyone—even your tour guide—to pose for photos. But general scenes of people and places are all right. To preserve military secrecy, it is forbidden to take pictures of bridges, tunnels and soldiers.

I'd like a film for this camera.	wǒ yào zhe-zhong zhào-xiàng-jǐ de jiāo juǎn	我要这种照像机的胶卷
black and white	hēi-bái de	黑白的
colour	cǎi-sè de	彩色的
colour slide (transparency)	cǎi-sè huàn-dēng-piàn	彩色幻灯片
May I take your picture?	wǒ néng gěi nǐ zhào zhāng xiàng ma	我能给你照张像吗?

PLANNING YOUR TRIP

Until recently the options open to the traveller to China were fairly limited. Now 148 cities and scenic spots are open to foreign visitors, itineraries are varied, and specialist tours provide interesting alternatives to the usual tourist destinations. Independent travel is increasingly accepted by the Chinese authorities.

Group Travel

Many tour operators in Europe and the United States offer group tours to China. The cost usually includes flight, full board accommodation in China, excursions, internal travel in China, services of local guides and interpreters and probably a couple of nights' stay in Hong Kong at the end of the trip. Groups consist of between 12 and 50 people, and the tour follows a fixed itinerary that takes in three to six cities. The duration of the trip may be from eight days to three weeks.

Be prepared, though, for last-minute changes in itinerary and pre-planned activities. Most tours cannot be sure of the exact agenda until arrival in China (and sometimes not even then). Visits to communes, factories, hospitals and schools as well as to historic and scenic locations are organized. Evening entertainment may include film shows, ethnic dancing or Chinese opera.

Special Interest and Adventure Tours

Alternative itineraries—but still in group format—are available for travellers with specialist interests—from acupuncture to archaeology. On these tours some time is spent in meetings with professional counterparts or visiting relevant institutions or sites. For those with a yen for adventure, some tours feature camping, trekking, mountain climbing, wilderness exploration and cross-country cycling, organized in conjunction with the China Sports Service Company.

Independent Travel

Those travelling independently will have more opportunity to wander off the beaten track—keeping in mind the sensibilities of the Chinese and the political climate.

To obtain a visa you should contact your local specialist tour operator who will apply to the Miscellaneous Department of the Head Office of CITS for authorization. On arrival in China you will be met by a Luxingshe guide, who will accompany you to your hotel and, if necessary, make arrangements for your onward journey.

Cruise Ships

Chinese ports are now popular stops for luxury cruise ships on round-the-world voyages, as well as for various regional carriers. Among the favourite destinations are Guangzhou (Canton), Shanghai and Xingang (the new harbour of Tianjin, the port nearest to Beijing). Other tourist ports include Xiamen (Amoy), Qingdao, Dalian and Yantai. Cruise ship companies sometimes offer their passengers excursions by rail or air; you leave the ship in one city and pick it up a couple of days later at another, spending the intervening time sightseeing inland—at extra cost, of course.

POLICE *(jǐngchá)*

See also EMERGENCIES. Armed police wear green uniforms and peaked caps displaying the national insignia of China. Tourists commonly confuse the police with members of the air force, who wear an indentical uniform except for the red star on the cap.

PRICES

Prices for tourist accommodation, meals, sightseeing and entertainment bear no relationship to the local cost of living. Goods and services priced on the Chinese scale represent considerable bargains for visitors. To give you a rough idea of what to expect, following are some approximate figures—subject to regional, seasonal and inflational variations.

Airport transfer. Taxi Beijing airport to city 32 yuan; airport departure tax 10 yuan.

Car and driver. 35 yuan per day plus 80 fen per kilometre.

Cigarettes (per packet of 20). Chinese 1.50 yuan, imported 2 yuan.

Entertainment. Theatre or Chinese Opera 2 yuan.

Hairdresser. *Woman's* haircut 2 yuan, shampoo and set or blow-dry 8 yuan. *Man's* haircut 6 yuan.

Hotels (double room with bath). Luxury international class 200 yuan. Moderate 70 yuan.

Meals and drinks. Lunch in moderate restaurant 10 yuan, in expensive restaurant 30–50 yuan. Imported spirits 2 yuan per drink, local spirits 1 yuan.

Museum entry. 10 fen – 3 yuan.

Transport. *City bus* 5–20 fen. *Taxi* Beijing railway station to Tian An Men Square 3 yuan; Beijing Hotel to Temple of Heaven 4 yuan.

PUBLIC HOLIDAYS

Offices and factories close on only four public holidays:

January 1	New Year's Day
January or February	Spring Festival (Chinese New Year)
May 1	Labour Day
October 1	National Day

The Spring Festival, determined by the lunar calendar, lasts for three days and is primarily a family holiday.

Other holidays, of modern origin, have little effect on daily life:

March 8	Women's Day
May 4	Youth Day
June 1	Children's Day
July 1	Communist Party Founding Day
August 1	Army Day

RADIO AND TELEVISION

Whether or not you understand Chinese, you may be interested in getting a glimpse of the state-run television. Features include the Chinese equivalent of soap operas, news bulletins, Chinese operas, films, sports events, and even some advertising. Most hotels provide television, individual or communal. A few hotels offer closed-circuit broadcasts of foreign-language programmes for tourists.

If you want to keep up with world events, you'll need a short-wave radio. In most parts of China a transistor set can pick up the BBC World Service, Voice of America or Radio Australia.

RELIGIOUS SERVICES

Many houses of worship that were closed, damaged or destroyed during the Cultural Revolution have now been restored to use. Services are again held at the Roman Catholic cathedral and the Protestant church in Beijing. If you wish to attend a religious service, give your guide advance warning so your request can be accommodated in the general schedule.

At what time is Mass/the service?	Shén mo shíhou zuò mí-sã/zuò lǐ bài	什么时候作弥撒/作礼拜?

RESTAURANTS *(fàn-guǎn)*

Inertia may push you towards your hotel restaurant—near at hand, predictable, with a menu in a sort of English and waiters who understand a foreigner's doubts and fears. They may even lay out knives and forks. But even if the hotel food is good, you're missing the adventure of a *real* Chinese restaurant. Considering the importance the Chinese have always attached to eating well, you can expect plenty of choice and the possibility of great gourmet experiences.

As you travel through the country, look for restaurants specializing in regional dishes—Peking duck in Beijing, seafood in Shanghai, and, if you're up to it, snake in Guangzhou. Your guide or hotel clerk can advise you in choosing a restaurant, probably rich in traditional atmosphere, or perhaps charmingly utilitarian. If it's the high season, or if you have a large group, it's wise to have someone phone ahead for a table.

The government permits the operation of some small private restaurants, in order to extend the facilities available to the people. The service is usually better than in state-run restaurants, but not necessarily the quality of the food.

When to eat

Hotels serve breakfast, Western-style and Chinese, from 7 to 8.30 or 9 a.m., later in the far west to compensate for the time difference. Breakfast is the only meal which normally offers a choice of Western-style and Chinese food.

Lunch is served from noon to 2 p.m.

Dinner is eaten earlier than in most Western countries — from 6 p.m. to 8 or 8.30 p.m. Even banquets in China start early and finish by 9 or 10 p.m. Some of the big hotels have restaurants which open after hours, for those who can't adapt to the Chinese timetable.

Asking the waiter

Could we have a table?	néng gěi wǒmen yī zhāng kōng zhuōzi ma	能给我们一张空桌子吗?
The bill (check), please.	qǐng kāi zhàng-dān	请开帐单。
I'd like ...	wǒ yào ...	我要……
beer	pí-jiǔ	啤酒
chicken	jī	鸡
fruit	shuǐ-guǒ	水果
fruit juice	guǒ-zhī	果汁
green tea	lǜ-chá	绿茶
jasmine tea	mò-lì-huā chá	茉莉花茶
mineral water	kuàng-quán-shuǐ	矿泉水
noodles	miàn-tiáo	面条
pork	zhū-ròu	猪肉
rice	mǐ fàn	米饭
vegetables	shūcài	蔬菜

Reading the menu

竹笋	*bamboo shoots*	sǔn
洋葱烧牛肉	*beef with onions*	yáng-cōng niú-ròu
蔬沙拉	*salad*	shūcaila
鸡汤面	*chicken noodle soup*	jī-tāng miàn
蘑菇鱼片	*fillet of fish with mushrooms*	mó-gū yú-piàn

栗子烧子鸡	*chicken with chestnuts*	lì zǐ shāozǐ jī
炒饭	*fried rice*	chǎo-fàn
(北京) 烤鸭	*glazed (Peking) duck*	kǎo-yā
鱼翅汤	*shark's fin soup*	yú-chì tāng
担担面	*Sichuan-style noodles*	dàn dàn miàn
古老肉	*sweet-and-sour pork*	gǔ-lǎo ròu

TIME DIFFERENCES

T

Although China extends across the longitudes, there is only one time zone in the whole country. This simplifies airline and broadcasting timetables, though in the far west it causes the sun to rise and set at peculiar hours in some seasons. Standard time remains in effect throughout the year, at GMT + 8. The chart below refers to the period March/April to September/October, when many countries in the northern hemisphere move their clocks one hour ahead.

New York	London	**Beijing**	Sydney
7 a.m.	noon	**7 p.m.**	9 p.m.

TIPPING

The authorities strongly discourage the practice of tipping. But a small gift—perhaps a souvenir of your home country—would not go amiss in certain cases, for a guide who has been extremely helpful, for instance. If the gift is refused, don't insist.

TOILETS

The public toilets in towns and villages are not up to international standards, though a programme is under way to upgrade facilities set aside for foreign tourists. One suggestion: always carry tissues with you.

Where are the toilets?	cè-suǒ zài nǎr	厕所在哪里?
Gentlemen	nán (cè suǒ)	男厕所
Ladies	nǚ (cè suǒ)	女厕所

TOURIST INFORMATION OFFICES

China International Travel Service (CITS, also known as Luxingshe) is responsible for looking after foreign tourists in China. CITS has branches in all major cities of China as well as scenic resorts and ports of entry. Contact the head office at:

No. 6, East Chang'an Avenue, Beijing, tel. 557217

Overseas offices are maintained in:

Great Britain: China Tourist Office, 4 Glentworth Street, London, N.W.1, tel. (01) 935-9427

U.S.A.: China International Travel Service, Inc., 60 East 42nd Street, New York, NY 10165, tel. (212) 867-0271

Where is the Luxingshe office?	Lǚ-xíng-shè zài nǎr	旅行社在哪儿?

TRANSPORT

Domestic flights. Air service inside China is the monopoly of the national airline, the Civil Aviation Administration of China, better known by its initials, CAAC. In recent years, with the acquisition of new aircraft and the development of new airports, domestic air travel has become more comfortable. But echoes of earlier aviation eras persist in the use of ancient Soviet propeller planes for short flights and the dislocations the slightest weather problem can cause.

On-board service on CAAC internal flights varies greatly; refreshments may be served and souvenirs are distributed.

Trains. The backbone of the Chinese transport network is the railway, which serves all major cities and tourist centres. Although the average speed is very slow, a voyage on a Chinese train can be an enjoyable and enlightening experience.

Express trains cost more than regular service, and sleeping berths are extra. Foreigners in any case must pay an additional charge. Seating is divided into "soft" and "hard" categories. The latter is usually quite crowded. Loudspeakers frequently erupt in announcements or Chinese music, day and night; to reduce the inconvenience, look for the volume knob under the table in private compartments.

Those travelling first class—both Chinese and foreigners—have access to a separate waiting room at provincial railway stations. In Beijing, however, foreigners, regardless of the class of their reservations, may enjoy luxurious isolation from the crush of the masses.

Boats. Travelling through China by boat has its delights—the scenery, the comfort, and, of course, the relaxed pace. As for the pace, it's actually faster to go from Wuhan to Shanghai by river boat than by train. And cheaper. Ships link ports like Shanghai, Tianjin, Dalian and Qingdao, although the schedules may be inconvenient. Try to find time for a river or lake ferryboat somewhere along the way to experience the crowds and the atmosphere.

Taxis. Almost everywhere in China, taxis are best ordered through the hotel. They do not cruise the streets looking for passengers, nor are there taxi ranks. A restaurant or Friendship Store will call a taxi, but if you're out on your own sightseeing for a couple of hours, it may be wise to take a taxi and keep it waiting for you between stops—a relatively inexpensive investment in convenience. Taxi drivers usually insist on giving receipts; they do not accept tips.

Metro. China's first underground railway (subway), the Beijing Metro, carries more than 70 million passengers a year quickly and very cheaply. Each station is visibly quite different from all others by virtue of its colour scheme or the shape of the columns or lesser details. This makes it easier to recognize a particular stop. Station signs are written in Pinyin as well as Chinese characters. An underground mass-transit system is under construction in Shanghai.

Bicycle. Since you are surrounded by cyclists, it may occur to you to take to the road yourself, for sightseeing and exercise. In Beijing and a few other cities there are bicycle hire shops accustomed to dealing with foreigners. You have to leave your passport or a deposit as security.

I'd like a ticket to ...	wǒ yào yì-zhāng qù ... de piào	我要一张去……的票。
single (one-way)	dān-chéng-piào	单程票
return (round-trip)	shuāng-chéng piào	双程票
I'd like a taxi.	wǒ xiǎng yào yí-liàng chū-zū-qì-chē	我要一辆出租汽车。

WATER *(shui)*   **W**

Avoid tap water. Even the water supplied in carafes in hotel rooms may disturb sensitive stomachs. But you can safely drink the boiled water hotels provide in thermos flasks for tea-making. In restaurants bottled mineral water is available.

USEFUL EXPRESSIONS

Please.	qǐng	请
Thank you.	xiè-xie	谢谢你
Yes (correct)/No (incorrect)	duì/bú duì	对/不对
Excuse me (I'm sorry).	qǐng yuán liàng	请原谅
Help me, please.	qǐng-nǐ bāng-zhù wǒ	请帮助我。
I don't understand.	wǒ bù-dǒng	我不懂。
Do you speak English?	nǐ shuō yīng-wén mā	你会说英语吗?
Where is the ... consulate?	... lǐng-shì-guǎn zaì nǎr	……领事馆在哪里?
American	měi-guó de	美国的
Australian	ào-dà-lì-yǎ de	澳大利亚的
British	yīng-guó de	英国的
Canadian	jiā-ná-dà de	加拿大的
New Zealand	xīn-xi-lán	新西兰
Good morning (till 10 a.m.).	zǎo chén hǎo	早晨好
Good day, good evening, hello.	nǐ hǎo	你好
Good night.	wǎn ān	晚上好
Goodbye.	zài-jiàn	再见
How are you?	nǐ hǎo mā	你好
Very well, thank you.	hěn-hǎo xiè-xie	很好,谢谢你
And you?	nǐ-ne	你呢?
good/bad	hǎo/huài	好/坏
big/small	dà/xiǎo	大/小
cheap/expensive	pián-yi/guì	便宜/贵
near/far	jìn/yuǎn	近/远
old/new	jiù/xīn	旧/新
old/young	nián-lǎo/nián-qīng	年老/年轻
beautiful/ugly	hǎo-kàn/nán-kàn	好看的/难看的

NUMBERS

0	líng	零	20	èr-shí	二十
1	yī	一	21	èr-shí-yī	二十一
2	èr	二	22	èr-shí-èr	二十二
3	sān	三	30	sān-shí	三十
4	sì	四	40	sì-shí	四十
5	wǔ	五	50	wǔ-shí	五十
6	liù	六	60	liù-shí	六十
7	qī	七	70	qī-shí	七十
8	bā	八	80	bā-shí	八十
9	jiǔ	九	90	jiǔ-shí	九十
10	shí	十	100	yī-bǎi	一百
11	shí-yī	十一	101	yī-bǎi líng-yī	一百零一
12	shí-èr	十二	200	èr-bǎi	二百
13	shí-sān	十三	1,000	yī-qiān	一千
14	shí-sì	十四	10,000	yī-wàn	一万

SIGNS AND NOTICES

出口	*Exit*	入口	*Entrance*
电梯	*Lift (elevator)*	紧急出口	*Emergency Exit*
关	*Closed*	停	*Stop*
有人（在使用）	*Occupied*	推	*Push*
不准拍照	*No photos*	危险	*Danger*
请勿抽烟	*No smoking*	问讯处	*Information*
警报	*Warning*	不准入内	*No entrance*
拉	*Pull*	小心	*Caution*
男厕所	*Gentlemen*	预订	*Reserved*
女厕所	*Ladies*	死亡危险	*Danger of Death*
切勿入内	*Keep out*		

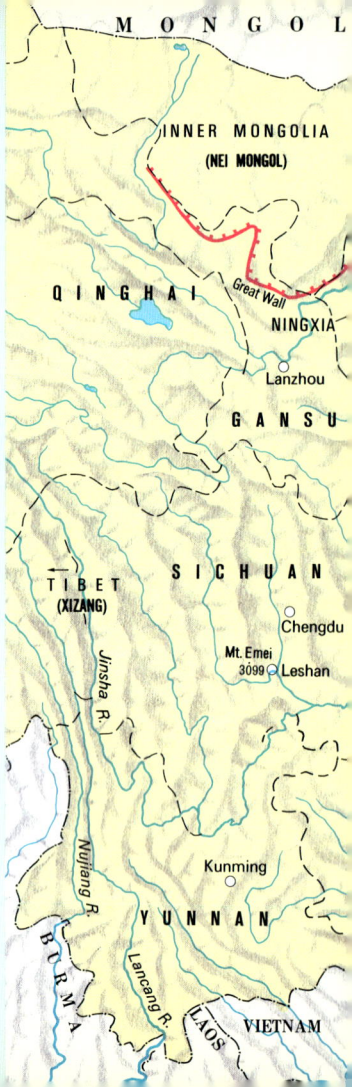

CHINESE PLACE NAMES

New and Old Spellings

Pinyin	Wade-Giles
Beidaihe	Peitaihe
Beijing	Peking
Chengdu	Chengtu
Chongqing	Chungking
Dalian	Dairen
Datong	Tatung
Fuzhou	Foochow
Guangzhou	Canton
Guilin	Kweilin
Hangzhou	Hangchow
Hohhot	Huhehot
Huang Shan	Hwang Shan
Jinan	Tsinan
Jingdezhen	Chingtehchen
Lanzhou	Lanchow
Luoyang	Loyang
Nanjing	Nanking
Ningbo	Ningpo
Qingdao	Tsingtao
Qufu	Chufu
Shanhaiguan	Shanhaikuan
Shenzhen	Shumchun
Shijiazhuang	Shichiachuang
Suzhou	Soochow
Tianjin	Tientsin
Wuxi	Wuhsi
Xiamen	Amoy
Xi'an	Sian
Yan'an	Yenan
Yantai	Yentai
Yangzhou	Yangchow
Yixing	Yihsing
Yueyang	Yoyang
Zhengzhou	Chengchow
Zhenjiang	Chenchiang

I A

Shenyang
Anshan

DEM.
PEOPLE'S
REP. OF
KOREA

Chengde

Baotou   Hohhot

Great Wall

BEIJING   Shanhaiguan
Beidaihe

low R.(Huang He)   Datong   Tianjin   Dalian

BO HAI

REP. OF
KOREA

HEBEI

Great Wall   Shijiazhuang

Yantai

Taiyuan   SHANDONG

YELLOW SEA
(HUANG HAI)

SHANXI   Jinan
1524
Taishan   Qingdao

Yan'an   Anyang   Qufu

Yellow R. (Huang He)   Kaifeng

Xi'an   Luoyang   Zhengzhou

Grand Canal

JIANGSU

0   200 km
0   200 miles

AANXI   HENAN   ANHUI   Yangzhou

N

Nanjing   Zhenjiang
Hefei   Wuxi
HUBEI   Wuhu   Shanghai
Yixing   Suzhou
Wuhan   Hangzhou
Huang Shan   Ningbo
1841

Yangtze (Chang Jiang)   Jingdezhen

ngqing   Yueyang   ZHEJIANG

Yiyang   Changsha   Nanchang   EAST CHINA
SEA
(DONG HAI)

HUNAN   JIANGXI

Fuzhou

IZHOU   FUJIAN

Taiwan Strait

Guilin   Xiamen   TAIWAN

GUANGDONG

GUANGXI   Conghua   Hot Springs
Guangzhou

Nanning   Foshan   Shenzhen

Taishan   HONG KONG
MACAO   (under UK Admin.)
(under Port. Admin.)

**MAJOR TOURIST
DESTINATIONS**

BEIJING

Donghuannanlu

SHOUDU (CAPITAL)
首都机场

Gongrentiyuchangbeilu

华侨饭店 Huadu
华侨 Hotel
建国饭店 Jianguo Hotel
友谊商店 Friendship Store
建国门外大街 Jianguomendajie
观象台 Observatory
火车站 Railway Station

Chaoyang-
menbeidajie

Ritanbeilu

Dongsishiqiao

Dongsibeidajie

Chaoyangmenneidajie

Overseas Chinese
Hotel 华侨饭店

Overseas Chinese
Building 华侨大厦

China Art Gallery

Heping (Peace) Hotel
和平宾馆

Dongfeng Market
东风市场

Peking Hotel 北京饭店

Dongchang'anjie

Xinqiao Hotel 新侨饭店

Chongwenmen Hotel 崇文门饭店

CITS 中国国际旅行社

Xizhaosijie

Xingfudajie

Guangqumenwaidajie

Guangqumenneidajie

Longtan L.

Dianmendongdajie

Drum Tower

Jingshanqianjie

Hall of Supreme Harmony
Palace Museum

Gate of
Heavenly Peace

Museum of the Chinese Revolution
Chairman Mao Memorial Hall
Museum of Chinese
History

Tian An Men Square
天安门

Dianmenxidajie

Jing Shan
Park

White
Dagoba

Bei Hai L.

Wenjinjie

Cultural Palace of
the Nationalities

Great Hall of the People

Monument to the People's Heroes
Bank of China

Zhengyang Gate

Beijing
Front Gate

Beijing
Roast-Duck
Restaurant

Zhushikoudajie

Hall of Prayer
for Good Harvest

Temple of Heaven
Park

Yongdingmen
neidajie

Qianmen Hotel

Yong'anlu

Beiwei Hotel 华北饭店

Beiweilu

Taipingjie

GREAT WALL (BADALING)
MING TOMBS

Xizhimenneidajie

Pindianxi-
dajie

Xisibeidajie Xidanbeidajie

Baitasidonglu

Fuchengmenneidajie

Xichang'anjie

Xizhaolu

Xuanwumenxidajie

Xuanwumen Hotel
宣武门饭店

Luomashidajie

Qianmen 前门饭店

Taoranting lu

Niujie

Guang'anmenneidajie

Baizhifangxijie

Minzu
(Nationalities) Hotel
民族饭店

Beilishilu

Nanlishilu

Sanlihebeidajie

Beijing Zoo

Chegongzhuangdajie

Yuetannanjie

Diaoyutai
Guesthouse
钓鱼台国宾馆

Yanjing Hotel
燕京饭店

Fuxingmenwaidajie

Lianhuachidonglu

Guang'anmennanbinhelu

246 SUMMER PALACE
FRAGRANT HILLS

LUGOUQIAO, ZHOUKOUDIAN

1 mile

1 km

Gongrenmenyuchangbeilu

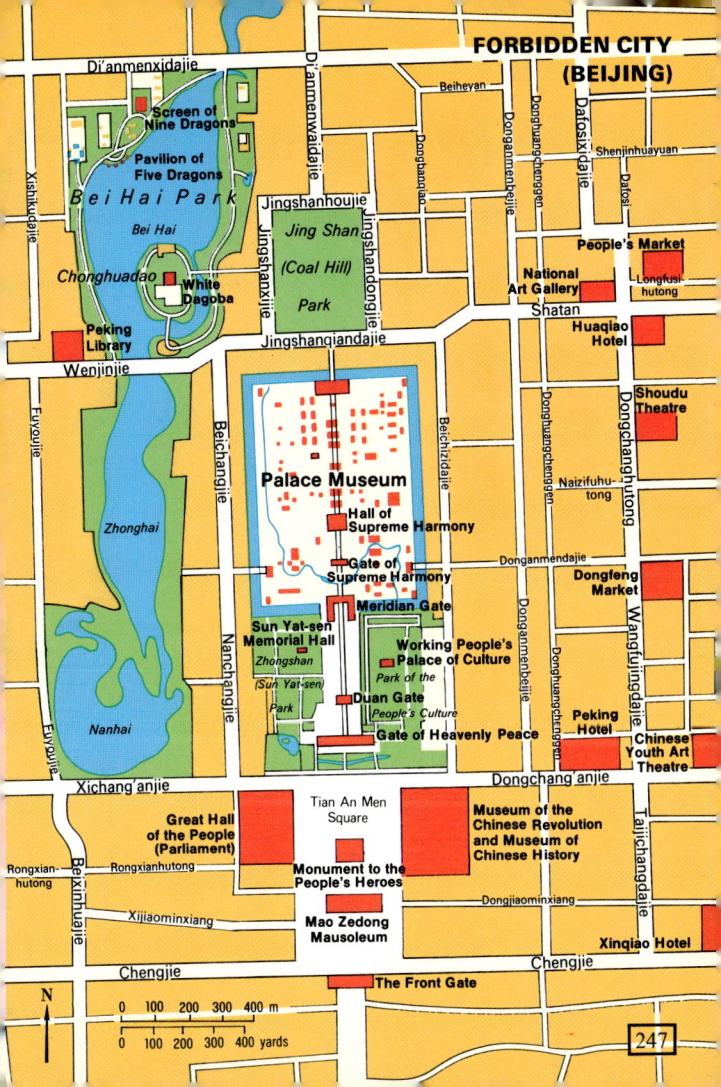

FORBIDDEN CITY (BEIJING)

Di'anmenxidajie

Beihexan

Di'anmenwaidajie

Dongbanqiao

Dongganmenbeijie

Dafosixijdajie

Shenjinhuayuan

Screen of Nine Dragons

Pavilion of Five Dragons

Bei Hai Park

Bei Hai

Chonghuadao

White Dagoba

People's Market

National Art Gallery

Dafosi

Longfusi-hutong

Jingshanhoujie

Jing Shan (Coal Hill) Park

Jingshandongjie

Jingshanxijie

Shatan

Huaqiao Hotel

Peking Library

Wenjinjie

Jingshanqiandajie

Donghuangchengen

Shoudu Theatre

Fuyoujie

Beichangjie

Beichizidajie

Palace Museum

Hall of Supreme Harmony

Naizifuhu-tong

Dongchanghutong

Zhonghai

Gate of Supreme Harmony

Donganmendajie

Dongfeng Market

Meridian Gate

Sun Yat-sen Memorial Hall

Zhongshan (Sun Yat-sen) Park

Working People's Palace of Culture

Park of the People's Culture

Donganmenbeijie

Donghuangchengen

Nanchangjie

Duan Gate

Peking Hotel

Chinese Youth Art Theatre

Fuyoujie

Nanhai

Gate of Heavenly Peace

Xichang'anjie

Dongchang'anjie

Wangfujingdajie

Great Hall of the People (Parliament)

Tian An Men Square

Museum of the Chinese Revolution and Museum of Chinese History

Rongxian-hutong

Rongxianhutong

Monument to the People's Heroes

Taijichangdajie

Xijiaominxiang

Mao Zedong Mausoleum

Dongjiaominxiang

Xinqiao Hotel

Chengjie

Chengjie

The Front Gate

N

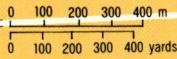

0 100 200 300 400 m
0 100 200 300 400 yards

247

CONGHUA

HUANGPU XINGANG

ERSHATOU

0   500 m

500 yards

Guangzhou Zoo

OUZHUANG

Xiaotielu

Zhongshanlu

Baiyun Hill Scenic Spot

Mausoleum of
the 72 Martyrs

Dongshanhu
Park

Xianlielu

Huanshidonglu

Dongfenglu

DASHATOU

Yan 4-lu

Pearl R.

Friendship Store
友谊商店

Luhu L.

Luhulu

Memorial Garden to the Martyrs
in the Guangzhou Uprising

Baiyun Hotel
白云宾馆

Guangzhou
East Station

Hongyunlu

Dongshalu

Museum of the Guangdong
Revolutionary History

Yan 3-lu

Huanghualu

Original Site of the Peasant
Movement Institute

Guangdong
Provincial Museum

Lux Xun Museum

Yanjiang 2-lu

Binjiang 2-lu

Fangcunlu

Guangzhou
Antique Store

Yuexiubeilu

Dengfenglu

Dongzhonglu

Zhongshanlu

ZHONGSHAN UNIVERSITY

Z

Beijinglu

Huaqiao (Overseas
Chinese) Hotel
华侨饭店

Guangzhou Hotel
广州饭店

Zhen Hai
Tower

Yuexiu Park

Dr. Sun Yat-sen
Memorial Hall

Jiefangbeilu

Yanjiang 2-lu

Bank of China

BAIYUN
白云礼机场

Guangzhou Station
火车站

CITS 中国国际旅行社
Foreign
Trade
Centre 中国出口商品交易会

Temple of the
Six Banyan Trees

Guangzhou-Foshan
Bus Terminal

Renmin (People's
Mansion
人民大厦

Binjiang 1-lu

China Hotel

Huaisheng
Mosque

International Telegraph
and
Telephone
Office

Dongfang
Hotel
东方宾馆

Guangxiao Temple
Guangdong Antique Store

Liuhua Hotel
流花宾馆

Renminbeilu

Renminzhonglu

Hepinglu

Liuhua
Park

Bus Terminal

Nanfang Mansion
南方大厦

Shuyinglu

Xiuli

Xicunlu

Xiutili

SHAMIAN

Guangzhou West
Station

Xinwulu

Shengli Guesthouse
胜利宾馆

Xiwanlu

Xiwanlu

Liwanlu

XICUN

Zhongshanlu

Dongfenglu

White Swan
Hotel 白天鹅宾馆

Xingfenglu

Xiuli

Guangzhou
South
Station

Xiangyanglu

Nanangonglu

Liwan Park

GUANGZHOU
(CANTON)

248

FOSHAN

Railway Station
火车站

Purple and Gold Mts.
(Zíjin Shan)

Linggu Pagoda

Dr Sun Yat-sen Mausoleum

Ming Emperor's Tomb (Ming Ling)

Zíjin Shan Observatory

Nanjing — Hangzhou Highway

Nanjing and Jiangsu Province Museum

Zhongshan Gate

Ruins of the Ming Palace

Wuchao Gate

Yudao Street

Nanjing Zoo

Xuanwu Lake

Beijing Dong Rd.

Dong Feng Rd.

Jiangsu Province Art Gallery

Dong Rd

Rujin Rd

Daguang Rd.

Communist Party Memorial to Delegation at Plum Tree Village

Daping Rd

Baizhou Park

Friendship Store
友谊商店

Zhongshan Rd.

Daqing Rd.

Drum Tower Department Store

Gulou Square 鼓楼场

Zhong Rd.

Shengli Jining I Hotel
胜利饭店

Jiangsu Hotel 金陵饭店

People's Market

Zhongshan

Historical Museum of the Taiping Heavenly Kingdom

YUHUATAI MARTYRS' MEMORIAL PARK

Jiankang Rd.

Zhongshan Rd

Zhonghua Rd.

Nanjing Hotel
南京饭店

Drum Tower (Gu Lou)

Beijing Xi Rd.

Antique Store

Chaotian Palace

Zhonghua Gate

YANGTZE RIVER BRIDGE

China International Travel Service
中国国际旅行社

Shuangmenlou Guesthouse
(双门楼)宾馆

Dingshan Guesthouse
丁山宾馆

Stone City

Pavilion of Victory at Chess

Mochou Lake Park

Rehetu Square
Baxi Hill

Zhongshan beilu
Zhongshanbeilu
Zhongxinglu
Danominglu
Zhongxinglu
Henanbeilu
Zhongxinglu
Baoshanlu
Sichuanbeilu
Tianmuxilu
**Railway
Station**
Tianmuzhonglu
Changshoulu
Changshoulu
Jade Buddha
Temple
Anyuanlu
Anyuanlu
Haininglu
Haininglu
Haifanglu
Haifanglu
Hengfenglu
Zhejiangbeilu
Henanbeilu
Wusong R.
Sichuanbeilu
Wusonglu
Kanding lu
Kangdinglu
Xinzhalu
Xinzhalu
Shimenlu
Shimenerlu
Xinzhalu
Beijingdonglu
Xinzhalu
Xinzhalu
Beijingxilu
Beijingxilu
① ②
No.1 Department
Store
Nanjingdonglu
Seamen's Club
④
⑤
⑥
Huangpu
Park
⑦
Nanjingxilu
Nanjingxilu
**Children's
Palace**
**Industrial
Exhibition**
People's
Park
⑧
**Municipal People's
Government**
Yananzhonglu
Weihailu
People's
Square
Jululu
Yananzhonglu
Jululu
Changlelu
Shanxinanlu
Shimenlu
Chengdulu
Jululu
Xizanglu
Yanandonglu
Zhongshandonglu
Huangpu R.
Zhongshandonglu
③
Changlelu
Jinlinglu
Jinlinglu
**Museum of Art
and History**
Renminlu
Jinlinglu
Huaihailu
Huaihailu
Maomnglu
Ruijinlu
Fuxing
Park
**1st. Nat.
Congress**
Huaihailu
Fangbanglu
Yuyuan
Garden
Fuyoulu
Fuyoulu
Henanlu
Guangxilu
Fuxingzhonglu
Fuxingzhonglu
Fuxingdonglu
Fuxingdonglu
Fuxingzhonglu
Yongjialu
Jianguolu
Jianguolu
**Cultural
Square**
Danshuilu
Chongqinglu
Zhongshandonglu
Jianguoxilu
Xiangyangnanlu
Shanxinanlu
Ruijinlu
Lijiabanglu
Liyuanlu
Zhonghualu
Zhaojiabanglu
Xietulu
Rumninlu
Xinzhaozhoulu
Nanchelu
Zhongshandonglu
Xietulu
Bansongyuanlu
N

SHANGHAI

250

1. Guoji (International)
   Hotel 国际饭店
2. Huaqiao (Overseas
   Chinese) Hotel
3. Jinjiang Hotel 锦江饭店
4. China International
   Travel Service 中国国际旅行社
5. Heping (Peace) Hotel 和平饭店
6. Shanghai Mansion 上海大厦
7. Friendship Store 友谊商店
8. Shenjiang Hotel 申江饭店

0   500   1000 m
0   500   1000 yards

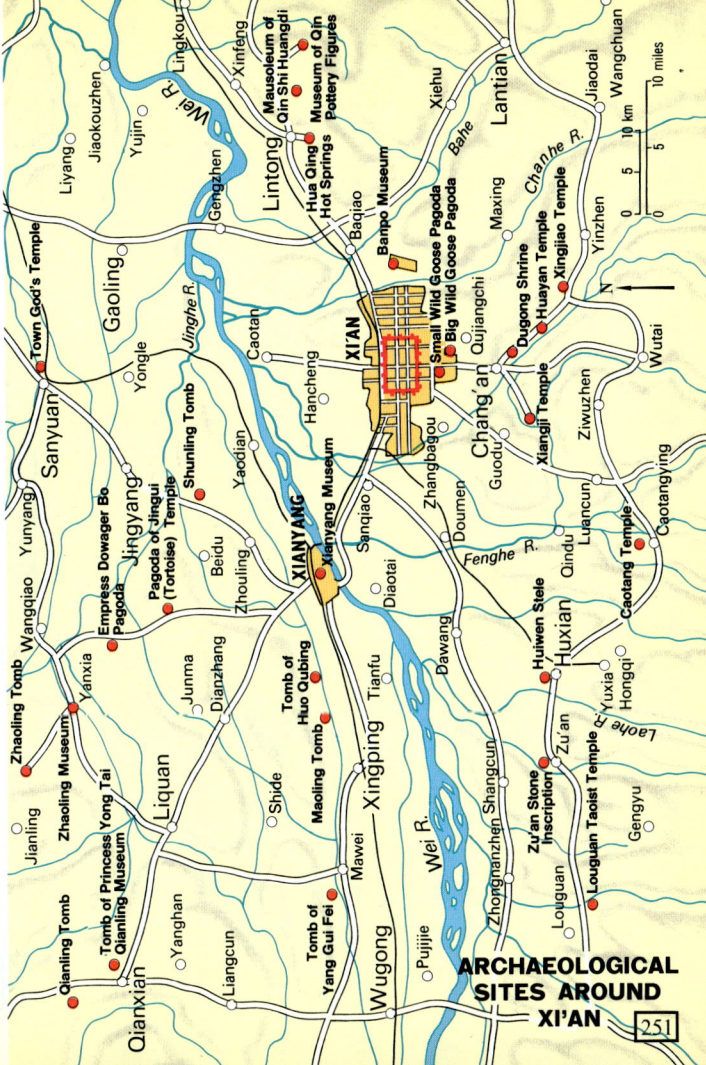

ARCHAEOLOGICAL
SITES AROUND
XI'AN

INDEX

An asterisk (*) next to a page number indicates a map reference. Where there is more than one set of page references, the one in bold type refers to the main entry. For index to Practical Information, see pages 216–217.